BROADCASTING
GETTING IN AND GETTING ON

JOHN MILLER

NEWPOINT PUBLISHING, LONDON

Published by **The Newpoint Publishing Company Limited**
Newpoint House
76 St James Lane
London N10 3DF
Tel: 01 444 7281
Telex: 265544 Answerback: Newpnt G
Telefax: 01 444 5825

British Library Cataloguing in Publication Data
Miller, John
   Broadcasting — Getting in and getting on.
   1. Great Britain. Broadcasting
   I. Title
   791.440941

   ISBN 0-86263-280-3

Typeset by: ATSS Ltd, Suffolk
Printed by: Werner Söderström Osakeyhtiö, Finland

To the memory of Kenneth Fawdry, who taught me so much at the outset of my broadcasting career.

Acknowledgements

In researching and writing this book I am indebted to countless friends and colleagues in many branches of broadcasting. Many of them are named and quoted in these pages, and I would like to thank them here for the patience and care with which they have all contributed, and commented on successive drafts of the relevant sections. In addition I am particularly grateful to Martin Gundry, Bob Nelson, Fiona Russell and Caroline Millington of the BBC, Sue Davis of the ITV Association, Greg Dyke of LWT, Chris Jelley of Yorkshire, Rod Caird of Granada, Ian Martin of Thames, Bob Duncan of Tyne-Tees, Janet Lee of the IBA, Dick Ross of the Royal College of Art, and Gary Crossley of West Surrey College of Art and Design, all of whom supplied me with invaluable detailed documentation.

Finally I must record my appreciation of the unstinting support I have received from my publishers, their care for detail, and their enthusiasm which sustained me through one particularly difficult period in the completion of this book.

Contents

List of illustrations

Foreword by Richard Hoggart

The start of John Miller's own career illustrates one fact which is not often appreciated: that the broadcasting organisations do not seek staff only or predominantly from Oxbridge. This is as true of the BBC as of the other institutions. The BBC may often be regarded as part of the Establishment, but has long and deliberately cast its recruitment net wide.

John Miller's university career underlines the main requirement of university or college applicants: simply to have a degree, even a very good degree, is not enough. You must have done much independent, innovative, extra-curricular work whilst studying for that degree. John Miller read politics at Nottingham but was, among much else, a leader in student drama activities.

He takes special care to point out that you don't need to have been in full-time higher education to apply for work in broadcasting: initiative is all, if it's of the right sort. And if you have been to university you might well gain from a spell in the outside world immediately after leaving.

Given his background, John Miller felt able to apply for one of the BBC's 'fast-track' openings, a General Traineeship. 300 applied that year and five, including John, got in.

Since then he has had a varied and rich career. First with the BBC; then with UNESCO in the Far East, helping to train broadcasters in Malaysia — this move shows his principled seriousness. Most other people would have stayed where they were so as not to miss possible promotion opportunities.

That same concern about the widest uses of broadcasting then led him to spend several years with the Open University, where he worked directly, happily and co-operatively with academics.

When the last main round of commercial television franchises came up he was tempted to the new company, TVS, to oversee their arts and education output. He has done that with notable success, some evidence of which is to be found in the books — one on Gielgud, one on An Englishman's Home — which have been spin-offs of a very full portfolio.

So John Miller is an extremely well-equipped guide for anyone wishing to enter broadcasting. His book has considerable merits. It is clear and entirely free from jargon; its tone is consistently helpful; it is both full and always practical. It successfully mixes straightforward factual advice with illuminating quotations from people in the business and, perhaps most interesting of all, gives revealing pen portraits of the careers of some of those who have markedly succeeded.

RICHARD HOGGART

Introduction

I seem to be asked by a growing number of young people, either in person or by letter: 'How can I get into broadcasting?' My experience is not unique, friends and colleagues in other branches of the business tell me the same story — their postbag has grown like mine. So when I was asked to write this book I knew there was a need for it.

The daunting part of such a task is the sheer breadth of the canvas, which in television embraces the BBC and the ITV companies, the growth of the independents with the success of Channel 4, the coming of satellite TV, and the possible effects on all of these of the Government's plans. The world of radio encompasses the BBC's domestic networks and the World Service at Bush House, and local radio in both the BBC and ILR.

Within that spread of potential employers I have also tried to cater for those of you with ambitions on either the production or the technical sides in their various specialist areas, and to give you some idea of the qualities necessary to succeed in them.

Broadcasting has always been a fiercely competitive field and the proliferation of channels and stations has been more than matched by the increasing number of applicants to work in them. For example, when I applied to join the BBC as a General Trainee in 1962 there were over 300 applicants, nearly a hundred of us were called for a preliminary interview, 19 of us reached the Final Interview Board, and five of us were appointed. In 1987 the equivalent numbers for what was re-named the Production Trainee Scheme were 1848 external applicants, 465 were invited for preliminary interview, 69 reached the Final Board, and 18 were selected. (There were in addition 90 internal applicants, two of whom were finally selected.)

That is the most competitive field of all, since the BBC has traditionally regarded all the successful candidates as potentially having a Director-General's baton in their knapsack, and most do end up as heads of departments or managing directors (Alasdair Milne was one General Trainee who did become D-G.)

In 1988 the Production Trainee Scheme was divided into three areas — television, radio and World Service — and for the first time the three areas were advertised separately.

Perhaps as a result applications increased appreciably over the previous year. For Television the number went up to 2200, for Radio it was 850, and for the World Service it was 650. The number of final appointments was about the same as in 1987, so the field is growing even more competitive.

In some areas you must have a degree, in others good GCSE and/or A levels, plus often an additional technical qualification (the relevant ones can be found elsewhere in this book). For all of them you will need unbounded enthusiasm for the medium of broadcasting, and a desire to communicate the knowledge or delight in whatever is the subject of the programme on which you are working. The hours are often long and unsocial, the working conditions can be hazardous or exposed to the mercy of the elements, so-called 'creative tensions' can sometimes lead to explosive confrontations, the financial rewards will not always seem commensurate with the skills or effort expended, but the job-satisfaction in most cases exceeds that of any other profession or industry I have come across in three decades of programme-making.

Above all, it is a collaborative medium. The size of the teams varies in the light of the respective technical and production requirements. An important radio interview may only need two or three people, the equivalent in television might need three or four times that number, while a television play could need 30 or 40 people in addition to the cast. Whatever the numbers none of them can do their job properly without the efforts of the others. Some of them will have worked together before, others meet for the first time in the studio or on location, but by the time the programme is finally 'in the can' everyone should, and usually does, feel part of that particular team.

Which leads me to the final and most intangible quality required to succeed in this demanding and strange business of ours — the right temperament. Applicants for most jobs in broadcasting find the interviews fairly stressful, but how you respond under pressure is just as important as whether you are well-read, highly intelligent, technically proficient, or have a good ear or eye. Sometimes decisions have to be taken in seconds — with no chance of considered after-thoughts — and they must be the right decisions. The ability to go into over-drive when the need arises and the adrenalin flows can be crucial. You may not know you possess it until it is demanded of you, and then it is a thrilling discovery. But if that ability eludes you, you are almost certainly in the wrong job.

One of the sharpest analogies I ever heard came from one of the most technically and editorially proficient producers I ever watched in action, Robert Siegenthaler of ABC News. In 1976 I filmed him co-ordinating their massive television coverage of the Republican Convention in Kansas City. Outside the Control Room he was the quietest and most courteous of men. On-air, driving a team of over 500 people, he was transformed into a human dynamo. He likened it to 'a 20-mule team, they trot and gallop, and some have to be encouraged and some lashed, and all of them pointed in the right direction, but they are all professionals and they do their job.'

What that job might be is what this book is all about.

JOHN MILLER

1

Getting in — the BBC

The first thing to decide is which general area you wish to work in — technical or production. In the former you would need to be at least 18 years old with normal hearing and colour vision, plus a good standard of education, typically GCSE English, maths and physics, plus in some areas study to A level in maths or physics; or English plus a BTEC National Certificate or Diploma in electrical engineering or electronics. In the latter you would probably need a degree for most (though not all) positions, the actual subject being immaterial except in very specialised areas.

If your eventual destination is television do not disregard radio as a means of entry. It was no accident that until 1988 BBC Production Trainees were sent on attachments to radio first to learn the broadcasting ropes before being thrown into the deep waters of television. A very high proportion of senior people currently working in ITV or BBC television began their careers in radio, and today many following them up the lower rungs of the ladder first climbed on in local radio.

It is also by no means one-way traffic. Many people move from television into senior positions in radio. One well-known name to do this is John Tusa, who began his career as a producer at Bush House, left to become a freelance presenter in radio (*The World Tonight*), and television (*Newsnight*), before rejoining the BBC staff as Managing Director External Services in 1986. John wrote and presented his first television series for me in BBC Schools Department, on 'Colonialism', and it was clear to me then that he had a glittering career ahead of him as a presenter and incisive interviewer, but I think neither of us guessed back in 1967 that he would end up on the Board of Management of the BBC.

It is also true that a handful of secretaries have eventually become distinguished producers, but I would not recommend any girl who wanted to be a producer to become a secretary first in the hope of promotion. Even if it comes, it is likely to be so long arriving that the frustration would become unbearable to most young women; and before I am accused of male chauvinist stereotyping let me hasten to add that at the time of writing it is still the case that virtually all secretaries, production secretaries, and production assistants in both ITV and the BBC are female, (though I should also add that the BBC is making strenuous efforts to live up to its description as an equal opportunities employer.)

On the technical side the gender ratio is changing, and prospects for women have improved. Although still in the minority, they are beginning to appear increasingly as audio assistants, and sound and camera operators, which were formerly almost exclusively masculine preserves; while for many years there has been a rough equality in the fields of graphics and set design, vision mixers, floor managers, and studio managers.

The BBC currently employs around 28,000 people to maintain the services on its two television channels, four domestic radio networks (and from August 1990 an additional Radio 5 for education and sport), the World Service (formerly known as External Services), eight major Regional Centres and fifteen smaller ones, and more than 30 Local Radio stations.

There are various means of direct entry to the BBC. The old Appointments Department has now been disbanded and its functions largely devolved to the Directorates. The training schemes are always heavily-subscribed. The job description for would-be Television Production Trainees for 1988 read:

'BBC Television wants to attract the brightest and most creative graduates or similarly qualified people, mainly to its factual programmes. We expect many of them will become future producers of programmes such as Panorama and That's Life, Tomorrow's World and Horizon, Wogan and Brass Tacks, Omnibus and Did You See, Food and Drink and Crimewatch — and whatever other output we develop in the whole area of non-fiction broadcasting. There are also a limited number of opportunities to progress to Drama and Light Entertainment.

'Initially we are offering a two year training experience starting in September 1988; six weeks of formal instruction leading to direct working experience on a number of programmes for the rest of the time. Trainees will have to generate programme ideas and argue their merits within a production team; and be able to demonstrate a willingness and effective practical ability to discover the information, people and locations which are the essential ingredients of any programme. Once training is completed, successful trainees can expect to compete for contracts or staff jobs as Researchers or Assistant Producers. Promotion to Producer, with full responsibility for initiating and directing programmes, can follow quite rapidly for the most promising trainees.

'Candidates should therefore be able to show that they are exceptionally well suited for this scheme. They will have a sharp original mind, an excellent degree and/or clear journalistic ability and experience, combined with a broad range of informed interests, creative flair and fresh ideas. Traditional background and success are less important than an awareness of the world and of the varieties of communities, tastes and beliefs within Britain.'

Candidates were asked to indicate their areas of interest:

Please indicate in order of preference (1,2,3, etc) the areas of programme making which interest you most. You need not mark all areas; do not mark any areas of no interest to you.
News & Current Affairs
General Documentaries
Religion
Science Programmes
Children's Programmes
Sport
Continuing Education
School Broadcasting
Drama
Light Entertainment
Music and Arts

This was followed by a large box in which to describe your viewing habits and explain your choices, and another in which candidates were asked to 'write a short critical review of a programme you have seen recently. In length and style it should be suitable for publication in a popular daily newspaper.'

A box was then left to write a *Radio Times* Billing:

Think of an idea for a programme which you would like to make. Think through how you would make it in case you are asked about it if selected for an interview. Then using the adjoining space and in not more than 60 words write the description of that programme which you would want published in Radio Times *as a billing to attract viewers, include details of the television channel, day and time of transmission you feel would be appropriate for your programme.'*

The equivalent box for Radio Production Trainees reads:

'Use this space to outline a 30-minute factual speech programme of any kind you would like to produce for Radio 4.'

The largest empty box on the Television Production Trainee form was headed:

'Please use the remainder of this page to give further details of your career, particularly media experience — formal or informal — activities and personal interests which you think will help us to assess your application.'

The wording on the same box on the Radio Production Trainee form is headed:

'WHY YOU? please use this space to give any information which you think makes you particularly suitable for this scheme.'

Although the wording on this last box changes slightly on different job application forms for the BBC, what you write in it can make all the difference to whether or not you get invited to the preliminary interview. In 1987 roughly a quarter of all applicants for the Production Trainee Scheme were seen, an encouragingly high proportion, but the three-quarters who fell at the first fence, filling in the form, failed to convince the reader that they had sufficient extra-special qualities.

Prospective employers, both BBC and ITV, are not just looking for academic skills. In any event, many of the applicants will appear equally qualified on paper. What they are seeking is evidence of initiative, flair, creativity, the ability to express yourself clearly and imaginatively, and organisational ability.

For many applicants the best opportunities to accumulate such evidence come at college, in the multifarious societies and extra-mural activities that flourish there. Someone who has held office and spoken regularly in the Students' Union or the debating society, directed or designed plays or operas, written for or edited the student newspaper, organised part of freshers' week, run the film or literary society, or any other creative activity, stands a much better chance of being interviewed than someone who merely joined a society or two without playing a major role — acting in someone else's production is much less valuable than directing your own. If, in addition, you have used your vacations to travel adventurously, or work in some mentally-stimulating or out-of-the-ordinary environment, then you would almost certainly reach the preliminary interview (and having lived and worked abroad plays a large part particularly in the selection of World Service trainees). Applications which mistakenly leave this last box on the form blank are put straight in the reject file.

Do not, however, interpret creativity as pure fabrication, you will very soon be caught out. Similarly, at the interview, do not pretend you have watched or heard a programme you may then be asked to criticise. But do try and make a point, in the days or preferably weeks before the interview, of immersing yourself in the programme areas you have specified as of particular interest to you. Do not hesitate to criticise a particular programme you have watched or heard, even if it came from your questioner's department, but do have some positive alternatives to propose as part of your criticisms.

The BBC's own comment on production trainees reads: 'The two commonest areas of weakness in otherwise good candidates were the inability to criticise constructively and the inability to turn ideas into real programmes. There are still some who apparently never watch television or listen to the radio....'

Some candidates for the World Service scheme, which has a strong current affairs requirement, had neither read a newspaper nor heard a radio news bulletin on the morning of their board. This did not make a good impression.

All the successful candidates in 1987 were graduates, 12 from Oxbridge and eight from redbrick universities. More than half were women. In 1988 at least one of the successful candidates was *not* a graduate, an indication that the pressure within the Corporation to broaden the range of recruits is beginning to have some effect.

Production Trainees undertake a series of attachments to different programme departments, varying in length from three to six months, and within two years must be successful at an internal Appointments Board to win a permanent job on the

Profile Television Production Trainee

Pratap Rughani joined the BBC in July 1988 at the age of 23. He was educated at Bancrofts School, Woodford Green, and Sussex University, with a year out between during which he sold china to Japanese and Americans and travelled extensively in India. At Sussex he read English in the School of African and Asian Studies, and was active in the drama and debating societies, co-editor of Union News, campaigned on third-world issues, was an NUS representative, and cut his broadcasting teeth on student radio and video projects. He broadened that experience as a radio reporter in Washington in one summer vacation, and working with Vietnamese refugees in Hong Kong in another, where he kept calling the South China Post to cover the story.

After a year's postgraduate diploma in newspaper journalism at City University (where he also wrote for *The Independent*) he applied for both the BBC News Trainee and the Production Trainee schemes, and was offered both. The first was looking for hard journalistic skills, the second for more general knowledge. He prepared by watching a lot of television, following *Newsnight* and *Channel 4 News* through a week or more, to observe and analyse the different news judgments; by working up a handful of solid programme ideas which he could expound and defend; and by writing and talking to as many Sussex graduates as he could find who were now in the BBC. The only question that floored him in the Final Board was: 'Where do we get the next performing dog for *That's Life*?' He believes he got the job because he had done extensive homework beforehand and held an interesting set of opinions. His evidence of initiative in so many spheres must also have been significant.

His first attachment was to *See For Yourself*, the BBC Review of the Year, as a researcher, then assistant producer on *Breakfast Time*, before spending five and a half months as a script editor in the Glasgow Drama Department for *The Play On One*, under Bill Bryden. He joined *Antenna* in the Science and Features Department in July 1989, and produced and directed his own films, writing his own scripts.

He has taken the one-month assistant producer's course, doing both film and studio directing, but when I spoke to him he had directed just one further multi-camera studio. He hopes initially to work in a Documentary Unit, and his future ambition is to edit a programme strand.

Profile **Radio Production Trainee**

Kim Normanton joined the BBC in September 1988 at the age of 26. She was educated at Bradford Girls' Grammar School, with a year between O and A levels at Topeka West High School as an educational exchange scholar. This American experience so impressed her that she decided to return there to continue her studies, and in 1982 she went to Principia College, Illinois, an independent liberal arts college, to read Spanish and creative writing. Like many American students she took a series of jobs in both term time and vacations to help pay her way, and still found time to act and produce musicals, co-ordinate a *Whole World Festival*, and tutor Cuban and Cambodian families. She feels the most important quality she acquired in the USA was the American 'go-for-it' approach to life, which brought out talents she did not know she possessed.

She returned to this country in 1985 and worked as a professional storyteller in schools (which she had first learnt to do in the States) and supplemented her income by acting as a tour director for American high school students on educational trips to Europe. Without any previous radio experience she managed to get some freelance reporting work for *Christian Science Monitor Broadcasting* in Boston which had just set up a London office. When she failed, however, to get work in local radio she decided she needed more training and took a one-year postgraduate diploma in radio and media studies at Highbury College, Portsmouth. This is where she really found her feet in radio, especially on the one-month attachment to BBC Radio Newcastle.

She prepared for her first BBC interview by listening to more Radio 4 than usual. When she passed that she took the second interview much more seriously and listened non-stop. Asked to identify her strengths as a producer on the application form she wrote it up as a radio feature. She thinks it is important at interviews to be what you are, not what you think they want. She did buy an interview skirt and advises: 'Dress comfortably, don't dress up, but don't be scruffy either.' Convinced her ideas got her the job, she says it helped that she had already made a radio feature during the Highbury course.

Her first attachment on joining was to *Woman's Hour*, making features and reporting, then Features, Arts and Education on a series called *In Their Element* under the very experienced producer Rosemary Hart. She had a difficult time next on *Loose Ends*, but loved her period with *You And Yours*. When we talked she had just finished her attachment to *WPFM*, a trendy teenage magazine and moved to *In The News*, a Schools Radio programme for 9-13 year-olds. She plans to stay in radio until she feels she has really learnt the business, and may eventually move to TV, or even go independent.

Profile World Service Trainee

Chris Bowlby went to the Royal Grammar School at Newcastle-on-Tyne, and took A levels in history, German and English. He took a year out between school and university on a youth exchange scheme in Berlin. At Christ's College, Cambridge, he read history and took part in college-based current affairs and journalism, and contributed occasionally to the University weekly newspaper *Stop Press*. He used the two long vacations to travel in Germany and Italy. After graduating he won a Kennedy Scholarship to Harvard (only 12 are awarded each year).

On his return he quickly lost interest in taking a PhD and got a job in the House of Commons Library, an experience which he believes was decisive in gaining him entry to the BBC as he learnt how to convey information impartially to MPs of all political persuasions. During his three years at the House of Commons he gained his first experience of radio by working on a feature on The Glorious Revolution of 1688 with a friend in the World Service.

He prepared for his first two BBC interviews by some concentrated listening and viewing, and every two or three days jotting down his thoughts and criticisms, which he then used as revision notes before each Board. For the second one he had to prepare and voice a two-minute profile of Yasser Arafat, Benazir Bhutto or Kurt Waldheim. With his specialist German knowledge he chose the third subject. He remembers being pressed hard on the news of that day and how he would handle it for radio, and in several cases being pursued intensively over some of his suggestions. He had identified a paucity of coverage of the North of England and only discovered subsequently that the World Service had just decided to set up an office in Manchester to remedy precisely that deficiency.

He joined the BBC in August 1988 at the age of 27, and was immediately sent on a seven-week radio training course which included a two-week journalism course. This was followed by two and a half months in Central Talks and Features at Bush House, scriptwriting and copy-tasting from the agencies' tapes; four months in Belfast on a live current affairs programme for the province; and six months in the African Service producing and reporting, where his French proved useful. Of all his attachments he felt most thrown in at the deep end in Belfast, but now values that intensive learning experience most highly. When I talked to him he was about to move on to the Current Affairs Department of the World Service, where he would start looking actively for a permanent job in the BBC, at Bush or Broadcasting House. He has no immediate plans to move into television, preferring to concentrate on mastering radio skills. He still hopes to travel and maybe work abroad, and to use both his languages more.

staff or more often these days initially a short-term contract of six months to a year. You are not expected to apply for a vacancy until well into your second year as a trainee.

NEWS TRAINEES

This scheme is similar to that for Production Trainees, but because of its narrower focus there are some important differences. It looks for reliable journalists for Network Radio and the World Service, and National and Regional television, working initially in newsrooms and production offices. In 1987 2000 people sent in for the application form, but only 642 were returned, probably because the more precise requirements demanded that the successful candidates were or became proficient in shorthand and typing before starting the course. (In 1988 both these numbers rose by about 100.) There were far more applications from women than men. 189 preliminary interviews winnowed out a short list of 50. Their final assessment was again slightly different from that for the Production Trainees. They had to take a written test, read to a video-camera a piece they had prepared themselves, and then face a panel interview with people drawn from News and Current Affairs Radio and Television, Journalist Training and Personnel. Those who fell at this hurdle failed to demonstrate more than a superficial knowledge of current stories, or a genuine interest and depth of understanding acquired over a longer period. Again the BBC lamented 'they also seemed to know little about News and Current Affairs Radio and Television programmes.'

Seven men and four women were finally appointed: three from Oxford, three from Durham, one from Exeter, one from Leeds, one from Sussex, one from York, and one from Central London Polytechnic.

News Trainees also undergo a two-year series of training attachments to different news programmes, and then have to compete at an internal Appointments Board.

LOCAL RADIO TRAINEE REPORTERS

Applicants for this scheme are sent an information sheet, an application form, a cassette, four news items and four press releases. In 1987 they were asked to write a news bulletin

Profile News Trainee

Jake Lynch joined the BBC in August 1989 at the age of 24. He was educated at two comprehensive schools, Healing near Grimsby, and Wintringham where he took his A levels. He began to read applied biology at UWIST, Cardiff but left after a term and a half to take his English A level, so he could read English at University College, Cardiff. This took him four years as he took a sabbatical after his second year to become the Student Communications Officer, handling all press relations for the Students' Union. He was also active in the other three years, writing occasional pieces for the student newspaper, regular theatre reviews for *The Morning Star*, playing football for the college, and acting, writing and directing student drama productions. He helped to adapt George Orwell's *Keep the Aspidistra Flying* which went on to the Edinburgh Festival.

After graduating he did a year at the Centre for Journalism Studies, also in Cardiff, during which he applied to the BBC. His advice on filling in the application form is to stress breadth of interest and experience, don't concentrate on journalism to the exclusion of all else. He had to do written tests while waiting for interview. These were in quiz form and he also had to take a subbing exercise in which he had to identify deliberate errors. He was asked to write background pieces for *Newsnight* to brief interviewers — two subjects he chose from a list were Dick Cheney and Winnie Mandela. He found the cross-examination was very thorough and designed to make him think on his feet; his interlocutors played devil's advocate with whatever he said. He felt they were looking for someone who could hold their own in an editorial meeting, assertive enough to put their point of view, and yet able to fit into what could be quite a large team. His postgraduate course equipped him well for fielding the direct questions about news content and analysis, but he also remembers being asked to comment on the recent changes to the *Nine O'Clock News*, with its fewer, longer items. A knowledge of current output was expected here, as in other departments.

On joining, he went on the initial 13-week training course for Network Radio, newswriting and newsgathering as for the Current Affairs Sequence Programmes; followed by a six-week mini-attachment at Radio Lancashire (half the length of the usual attachment). When I spoke to him he was about to go to TV Training for seven weeks, and expected to follow that with a three-month attachment to a Regional TV Centre, and two more mandatory ones in Network Radio and TV. He came in with an idee fixe of becoming a TV reporter, but his flair and preference is for writing, so he still has an open mind about his eventual ambition, although in the long term he fancies being a Correspondent either home or abroad.

and record it on the tape, and a two-minute interview with someone of their choice. The shortlisting this time was done solely on the basis of what was recorded on the cassette, without any reference at this stage to the application forms. 1138 applied, and 253 were given a preliminary interview. These were conducted at local radio stations throughout the United Kingdom, and the interviewers were looking for a commitment to local radio and to journalism. So they were disappointed to find that many candidates had not bothered to listen to the radio news on the day of their interview. More than that, 'some were quite surprised to be asked about their news listening even though they were applying to become a trainee radio journalist!'

60 people reached the final board and took a news test and a voice test as well as the interview. All of the 18 successful candidates already had some experience of local journalism, acquired at college or after, on their local paper or local radio station. At the initial application stage the men outnumbered the women by three to two, but by the final board it was almost exactly 50:50. The final selection was eleven men and seven women. The educational background for this group was much more varied. Only two came from Oxbridge, nine from redbrick universities, and the rest from Polytechnics. As it happened all the selected candidates were graduates, but the BBC commented that the standard of non-graduate applications was high. This continues to be true — in 1988 two of the 24 candidates who were finally appointed were non-graduates.

PERSONNEL TRAINING SCHEME

Although this scheme does seek people with experience of work and an interest in broadcasting, in practice the successful candidates do tend to come from the world of personnel administration. 1987 produced six recruits, from an initial application of 223. 98 were invited to a preliminary interview and test, and 24 of those to a final selection day at the BBC's Engineering Training Centre at Evesham, which comprised a panel interview, written tests and group exercise. At the beginning of the process the female applicants outnumbered the males by nearly three to one.Of the six finally selected, five women came from redbrick universities while the only man came from Manchester Polytechnic.

Profile **Local Radio Trainee**

Laura Dalgleish was 21 when she joined the BBC. She took her O levels at Lowther College, North Wales, and went on for seven terms to the sixth-form at Rydal School, Colwyn Bay. She took nearly a year off and went to Australia as a teacher for 10 months, before going to Nottingham University to read English from 1985 to 1988. She already had her eyes set on a broadcasting career, so spent most of her spare time at the University radio station, working firstly on the breakfast programmes and then on the news. She managed to squeeze in some writing for the student newspaper *Impact*, a little drama and music, and the annual charity event; but her greater priority was to gain some experience with the two local radio stations in the city, Radio Trent (ILR) where she worked on the Saturday sports programme, and Radio Nottingham (BBC) where she made a couple of features.

She believes that without this practical experience she might not even have been called for interview. The preliminary one was in Birmingham for just over 20 minutes with two people; and the final one was two months later in London with four interviewers for a little over 45 minutes, plus a 35 minute test — to put a bulletin together on paper, record a 40 second piece on one of four topics (she chose the US elections), and answer 10 questions. Both interviews demanded considerable speed of response, both theoretical to discover her news sense and political knowledge, and practical to discover how she would handle various topics. She had taken care to spend all day at Radio Nottingham before the interview so she was totally up to date with recent coverage, and had also compared the broadcasts of the rival ILR and BBC stations since she guessed rightly that the Board would be interested in the competition's approach and news values. She underlines the necessity of being very familiar with the output to demonstrate keenness, and the overriding importance of gaining practical experience of local radio by pestering the local station until they give you a chance to show what you can do. Indeed, she believes that without such experience, and a quality demonstration tape (which all applicants must submit), you are unlikely to be called for interview. She also thinks it is invaluable to talk to people who have previously been through such Boards.

On joining she did the standard initial 13-week training course in London which was practically based, and then did successive attachments to the local radio stations in Northampton (six weeks) and Bristol (initially for three months, but then she was appointed to the permanent staff there). When I spoke to her she was looking forward to consolidating her skills now she had finished her trainee period, and thought that she would like to move on to Network radio at some stage, and possibly to television in the longer term.

TRAINEE STUDIO MANAGER SCHEME

This has always been one of the larger group entry schemes to the BBC. Studio Managers are employed initially on the essential tasks of operating the control desks and edit-machines in radio studios right across the BBC, but have also always proved a fertile source of recruits for eventual radio and television producers. Many now distinguished names in both media began their careers as 'SMs' years ago, and the opportunities still exist for the new intakes to follow in their predecessors' footsteps.

The educational profile of 1987 applicants is significantly different from all those described above. Nearly two-thirds of the original applicants and nearly half of those finally selected had no degree-level education.

A higher proportion of candidates also succeeded than in any of the previously mentioned schemes. 693 applied, 380 were invited for preliminary interviews, 138 made it through to the final board and 59 were selected. Although far more men than women applied by a ratio of more than three to one, the final division was about one and a half to one.

Six came from Oxbridge, 26 from redbrick universities, two from polytechnics, and all the rest had no degree. Operational experience often proved more decisive than academic accomplishment, whether in hospital, campus, or local radio, though the BBC does look too for a real interest in the content of a broad range of radio programmes, as well as an awareness of their technical and artistic excellence. Personal initiative was its own reward here too: 'We were impressed by the determination some candidates had shown to acquire the basic knowledge they would need to handle the sort of technical questions they would be asked at interview, for instance taking O level physics in their own time.'

Although many of the successful candidates were in their early twenties the profile of the youngest is instructive: 'He is 18 and took A levels in maths, physics and chemistry in 1987. He built up and assembled his own hi-fi, and has been responsible for light and sound for school plays. His musical interests include singing and playing the violin and piano. He installed and ran a pupils' telephone system at school.'

In 1988 the numbers applying fell below 500, but the BBC commented that there was a higher proportion of realistic ones, and several took advantage of the advice given when they

Profile Studio Manager Trainee

Tanya Bhoola joined the BBC in January 1989 at the age of 19. She was educated at Gumley School, Isleworth, where one of her great interests was music, which she took at both O and A level. While still at school she learnt the basic production skills at an unlicensed radio station in Twickenham, a useful grounding when she started voluntary work on Great Ormond Street Hospital Radio (where she still helps out in her spare time). Despite pressure from her schools careers officer she was determined to go straight into radio without going to university first, as all the music degrees had a classical emphasis and her interest is in popular music. She advises applicants 'don't let anyone put you off what you really want to do.'

Her first Board seemed to be more of a personality interview, though she was expected to describe the differences between Radios 1, 2 ,3 and 4. The second pressed her more on news and technical questions. In addition to the normal hearing and colour vision tests she was given a high-frequency hearing test. Of the 15 successful candidates, Tanya was the only one without a degree (although her music qualifications were a significant advantage).

She began her training at Evesham on a two-month course of lectures with some studio experience in the basics of equipment, with multiple-choice tests, and ending with an intensive week when the whole course had to simulate Network programmes all day long. This was followed by six weeks of studio exercises in London, again ending with a whole week of Network simulations.

Tanya then went to the World Service at Bush House for three months, and after one week's training she worked unsupervised on news or talks programmes, or as the second SM on more complicated features. Next she was sent to Broadcasting House where she had two weeks' training before going to Magazine Programmes and then News and Current Affairs — she found the fast moving news sequences like *World at One* and *P.M* 'really scary' — before returning to Magazine Programmes. Her most demanding experience was the live news coverage of the IRA bombing of the Marine Band School at Deal.

She advises applicants to try and shadow an SM for a day or more before the interview to get an understanding of the job, to listen to all the radio channels, and to keep up with the news, especially on the day of the interview. She was able to answer 'What's the main news today?' with an update on the latest incident in Panama that was actually ahead of the Board's information.

When we met she had just passed her final operational test and become a member of the permanent staff. She hopes soon to work in Radio 1 and 2, and longer term she would like to have a go at presenting and producing music shows for these channels. She has no wish to move into TV, as she prefers sound to pictures.

failed to gain entry in 1987, and succeeded at their second attempt.

TECHNICAL OPERATIONS

This important part of programme production includes recording operators, audio assistants, camera and sound operators, and regional or news technical operators who are trained in a number of disciplines. The BBC looks for candidates with an abiding interest in the broadcast media, demonstrated by their involvement in some aspect of the audio-visual arts, such as hospital radio, amateur dramatics, or music, either in production or performance. What turns any operational job from a mere technical skill into an art is the creative use of those skills.

The training programme lasts for three years, beginning with an initial 10-week course at the BBC's Training Centre at Evesham. It includes an introduction to basic broadcasting techniques and some instruction on equipment relevant to the particular area of work. The course ends with both practical and written tests which must be passed before going on to gain practical on-the-job experience. Work and progress is assessed at the end of the first year, and if it is satisfactory the appointment is confirmed. Training on-station continues for another two years, with a four-week course in the final year on the more advanced techniques of the particular job. Successful completion of this training programme makes you a qualified operator.

Would-be camera operators will need to show evidence of their interest in the visual arts, especially photography. Sound operators work in studios and on location, and to capture the right sound for a particular production they need to understand the characteristics of the microphones and recording equipment, and to develop a practical approach to solving problems.

Trainee recording operators work in the telecine and videotape areas, from initial recording through editing and post-production, which these days also requires a familiarity with various special-effects techniques.

Operators in the regions are expected to develop a more comprehensive range of skills, since they could be called on to work on cameras or sound or, in conjunction with an engineer, testing and aligning studio equipment prior to transmission. News technical operators are similarly called on to work on a wide range of different activities.

In considering applications for all these posts, the BBC is not looking for professional experience or expertise, but some tangible expression of the depth of interest in a particular aspect of broadcasting. The creative instinct is difficult to measure, but it is the quality they will be seeking to identify at the interview.

ENGINEERING

The Engineering Division runs the most structured entry and training schemes in the whole of the BBC, and since the two are so interlinked it is simpler and clearer to outline both as a single process, as you would experience it. There are three separate routes of entry.

Trainee engineers

You may apply at the age of 18 if you have studied to A level. The minimum requirement is GCSEs in English, physics and maths, plus study to A level in maths and physics, or English plus a BTEC electronics Diploma including level III maths. The full training period lasts for about two and a half years, including three packages of three months each in residential training at the BBC's Engineering Training Centre at Evesham for the A, B, and C courses. Normal colour vision and hearing are essential, and applicants are required to be tested for both.

Each of the BBC Directorates recruits its own intake — Television, Radio, World Service and Monitoring, Transmitters, and the various Regional Centres. About 35 a year go to Television, 20 to Radio, about a dozen to the World Service, 20 to Transmitters, and 10 to the Regions.

Most people's first day is at Evesham for the A course — an introduction to BBC practices and a thorough revision of what the students have learnt in their previous studies. This course is rigorously assessed, and you have to pass it to stay in the BBC. The failure rate is around 25 per cent. Trainees then undergo further training at their respective stations and studying by means of the Training Books. On completion of approximately 12 months' service they return to Evesham for the B course on BBC equipment, digital systems, computer theory, computer practices, and modern technology. The increasing speed of technical change means that this syllabus is almost constantly being revised and updated. This is a two-part course, with periodic testing, and Part One must be completed successfully before commencing Part Two. Anyone who fails the B course may have their contract terminated.

Within 9 to 15 months of successfully completing the B course, there is a requirement to commence a third period of training. The C course is in two parts, those who complete it successfully join the 'reserve' of their parent Directorate at the end of the 'statutory training'. Again there are tests and assessments made throughout the course, and successful completion of Part One is necessary before moving on to Part Two. And there will still be specific training later on specific equipment.

Direct-entry engineers

This is open to people with an engineering or electronics degree or equivalent qualifications such as a BTEC HND. The training period here is about a year in duration. Like the Trainee Engineer course described above, it is essential here too to pass the C course at the end of training, and to have good reports.

Graduate trainee engineers

This is a fairly recent innovation by the BBC. Because of the nationwide shortage of electronics engineers it was necessary to cast the net wider for potential recruits, so this scheme is open to all graduates without an electronics degree. It proved immediately successful, attracting nearly 9000 applications when it was first advertised. In 1989 there were 1200 applications, and nearly 50 were appointed. It has also produced a higher percentage of women applicants and final selections.

The selection system follows the familiar three-stage routine — application forms, preliminary interviews of about half an hour for technical questions, and a final interview Board of about 40 minutes. Between 5 and 10 per cent of initial applicants are finally offered a post.

But it is worth emphasising that the greater shortage of suitably qualified engineering candidates, compared with the non-engineering side, offers better chances for those who are well-qualified. It is *not* common, however, for people to move from engineering into production.

Profile Direct-Entry Engineering Trainee

Dharmesh Kanadia joined the BBC in July 1989 at the age of 25. He was educated in London at Somerset Secondary School for his O levels, then at Waltham Forest Technical College for his HND. He was unemployed for a year before going to North London Polytechnic to take a degree in electrical and communications engineering. He was a member of the Asian Society, but much of his spare time was spent working as a motor mechanic. His initial BBC interview was on 'the Milk Round' where BBC staff visit colleges, polytechnics and universities. This was very informal with just one person, and much of it centred on his project — designing a video fader unit. The second interview was by five people, including his first interviewer, and very technical. He was again questioned about his project, and he remembers that the whole of the 45-minute Board was very thorough and needed quick responses. He was given a circuit diagram and asked to draw various solutions.

He has always had a deep and practical interest in the workings of television and videos, and this stood him in very good stead when he was asked about his understanding of the PAL TV system. By now he also had a lot of non-BBC interview experience, so was less nervous than he might otherwise have been.

His first two weeks were spent observing in SCAR (Spur of Central Apparatus Room), TAR (Technical Apparatus Room), OBs at Parliament and AMR (Advanced Maintenance Room). Then he went on the four-week A course at Evesham, followed by six weeks on-station training at Television Centre in London. He was offered the choice of any department and chose AMR. After five weeks on the B course at Evesham, he returned to AMR with a log book to complete for the different areas.

He believes his interests got him the job more than his qualifications, as none of his friends succeeded who were often better qualified than he was. His advice is to show evidence of a particular interest in television by choosing TV courses at college, picking a project in the broadcasting field, visiting the Institution of Electrical Engineers and attending their lectures on television. He wishes more Asians like himself would apply to the BBC since he is impressed how seriously it takes its obligations as an Equal Opportunity Employer. In his year there were about an equal number of entrants from universities and polytechnics. He also believes keen applicants should keep applying even if they fail at first, and gain useful and relevant extra experience in the interim; he knows of more than one colleague who failed at the first attempt, and succeeded at the second or third. He looks forward to all the technical developments fast approaching in the '90s, and feels 'spoilt for choice' in the opportunities open to him.

OTHER ROUTES

In addition to the broad categories of traineeships described already, the BBC also advertises vacancies for particular grades and skills, such as secretarial, make-up, or graphics artists; or specific departments, like Children's, Sport, or Light Entertainment (LE). These are usually at the lower levels. For LE or Drama, for example, it may well be at the level of floor assistant or assistant floor manager, you would have to be over 21 and would probably need to have had experience backstage in the professional theatre. Other specialist qualities needed for other specialist departments will be looked at later in this book.

Advertisements for these direct-entry vacancies appear in the *Guardian*, *Independent*, *Daily Telegraph*, *Times*, *Sunday Times*, *Observer*, *Broadcast*, and the ethnic press. Those for News Trainees appear in the *UK Press Gazette*. Particular vacancies outside London are sometimes advertised only in the local press.

Every year the BBC recruits around 3000 people from outside, ie about 10 per cent of its total staff. In 1988 there was a total of about 21,000 applications for all the various trainee entry schemes, and in addition over 90,000 unsolicited applications for jobs that were not even advertised — letters and telephone calls merely enquiring what vacancies might arise. Every BBC post that is currently advertised externally can be found on CEEFAX (Page 295). It is BBC policy to give preference to internal applicants over external candidates, which is why only about 30 per cent of all BBC vacancies are advertised outside; the other 70 per cent are restricted to internal applicants, but the latter description does of course include short-term contract staff, so even a temporary job with the Corporation opens up the opportunities for advancement.

There are two other important general points to make about recruitment to the BBC before we turn to the alternatives. The first is that the best point of entry is rarely straight from school, and not all that frequently straight from university or other college, except in engineering. A spell in newspapers, publishing, advertising, the theatre, travelling or teaching is more likely to give you that edge of experience or self-confidence when you are competing against your peers.

The second is that you should no longer regard it, as many people did until recently, as a job for life with the same employer until you retire at 60. Movement in and out of the BBC is at a higher rate than it has ever been, some of it voluntary and some of it involuntary, for economic as well as creative reasons, so we should now turn and examine the alternative options.

2

Getting in — ITV

There are over 15,000 people working in Independent Broadcasting for the 15 ITV regional contractors, TV-AM, ITN, Oracle and the Channel Four Television Company. (Nearly another 2000 work for the Independent Local Radio stations, who will be described in greater detail later.) So the total is just over half the entire BBC strength.

There are a number of major differences between the ITV system and the BBC — most importantly its federal structure and its system of financing through advertising — which have a direct bearing on its policies of recruitment and training.

The size of the regional companies varies considerably, from Channel Television which employs about 100 people, up to Thames which has a staff of nearly 2000. (The full list of ITV companies and their addresses to write to can be found at the back of this book.) But it is probably worth spelling out that the 15 regions fall roughly into three divisions in terms of size, income and responsibilities. The five Majors are Central, Granada, LWT, Thames and Yorkshire, and their name means that they are required to make the major contribution to the ITV Network in prime time, ie 7.00-10.00 pm. There are then five large Regional companies, Anglia, HTV, Scottish, TVS, and Tyne Tees. Finally there are five much smaller Regional companies, Border, Channel, Grampian, TSW, and Ulster, which serve the most sparsely populated areas of the UK. The five Major Programme Controllers and two from the Regionals (Scottish and TVS) draw up the network schedule.

You do not have to be a resident of the region when applying for a job with the ITV company for that region. It obviously helps in certain special fields to be a native if you are applying in Scotland, Wales or Northern Ireland, though it is also noticeable that there are, for example, a number of Scots in senior positions in several of the English companies. But the only formal restrictions on employment by geographical origin are to be found in the Channel Islands, and there the restrictions on residence and work permits are imposed on the broadcasters by the Islands' authorities, as on every other employer there.

Apart from that, the only other extra hurdle for would-be entrants to ITV has been the requirement at certain levels in some companies to be already in possession of the appropriate union ticket — the Association of Cinematograph, Television and Allied Technicians (ACTT), the National Union of Journalists (NUJ), etc. Some of the colleges that run courses for students who wish to work in broadcasting have negotiated special accreditation agreements with the ACTT for the union ticket to be granted on successful completion of the course (these are indicated at the back of this book). The recent upheaval in the structure and working practices of ITV means that these conditions and requirements are being constantly renegotiated, and now vary considerably from company to company.

In the early days of ITV it was always accused of poaching its skilled employees from the BBC. Although it still remains true that the BBC's greater size enables it to take on a higher proportion of people without experience and train them up than is possible for an individual ITV company, many of the latter now do run quite sizeable recruitment and training schemes of their own. Central, for example, which took over the Midlands franchise from ATV in 1982, has since then developed more than 100 employees across the company in a range of jobs. It currently has around 2000 people on the staff and several hundred more on contract. Because of the company's standing it tends to recruit people with specialist skills and an already-proven track record, so the contract employees tend to be largely a floating population, who come in and out for specific projects, for a few months at a time.

Central does not have a policy of recruiting trainees on a regular basis because, unlike the BBC, it does not have a set annual intake. Nor does it recruit school-leavers because most of the available posts are best suited to mature graduates each year, two or three for management or sales training (usually people with a background in accountancy) and two as newsroom trainee journalists. The latter scheme was suspended for one year in 1988 because, according to Bob Southgate, Deputy Director of Broadcasting at Central, 'one effect of the success of the training scheme was a lowering of the average age of the newsroom staff to a level which began to cause concern'. This pause was an interesting exception to a marked trend in other programme areas towards favouring youth over experience.

Bob Southgate makes the additional point that 'although other trainees are accepted for a wide range of technical jobs there is no discernible pattern and no set quota — recruits are simply sought as the need arises'. That policy is fairly typical of all the ITV companies. Vacancies are generated either by departures of existing staff, or a change in emphasis in production in favour of one area over another. When TVS decided to increase its output of light entertainment programmes for the ITV Network in 1988 it brought in a number of extra production staff, the great majority on short-term contracts.

There are however, some exceptions to this general rule. In 1987 LWT recruited two trainee managers, three apprentice electricians, and one apprentice carpenter on a speculative basis; and raw recruits from outside joined as trainees in the Camera and Sound departments. LWT also has an industrial placement or work experience scheme. Its Market Research Department usually has at any one time a university student working in the area. The Sales Department in 1988 invited applications from selected universities and polytechnics for a small number of students to work in that area, covering a period of one man-year between them (or one person-year as LWT would probably prefer to put it). The Production Division invited about a dozen students from the Ravensbourne College of Design and Communication to join both the Production and the Production Engineering Departments for a period of six weeks, to observe and have 'hands-on' experience. Other 'shadow' visits are arranged, on a less formal basis, ranging from one to four weeks in all divisions of the company, mainly supplied from schools in London with pupils who require short-term work experience.

Yorkshire runs a similar scheme of student placements for those living or attending college within YTV's transmission area. It is not open to school children, only students following a higher education course connected with either the media in general or one of their departments in particular. The attachments can vary between one day or two weeks, but are usually for no more than one week. The value of these rather ad hoc arrangements depends on the amount of pressure on the relevant department at the time.

There is also some movement in the other direction. LWT

has sent a number of its vision-mixers on a new 'score reading' course, organised by TVS which has for some years specialised in music programmes, especially in the classical and operatic fields. That kind of inter-company collaboration has become increasingly common in recent years. The ITV Association (formerly known as ITCA), the co-ordinating body for the television companies, runs about 100 courses a year, mainly in response to their collective and individual requirements. These include those for directors run in conjunction with Bristol University, HTV and TVS, and the Graduate Editorial Trainee Scheme.

The ITV Association decided many years ago that establishing its own training school would not be cost-effective, and that a better policy would be to send its trainees to a variety of independent institutions, with their own specialisms to offer. Its support takes three forms: it pays the full course fees for all trainees it sends; it gives substantial grants to the colleges concerned; and quite often it donates the actual equipment to be used as well as cash. Much the biggest beneficiary is the National Film and Television School at Beaconsfield for a broad range of full-time and short courses — in 1988 it received over half a million pounds from the ITV Association. Smaller sums went to Ravensbourne College of Design and Communication (to equip its short courses and two-year BTEC HND courses), to Bristol University, and to the Actors' Centre to help run its short courses for Equity members on acting for television. (Actors as such fall rather outside the scope of this book, but some of their skills are also important to presenters on radio and television, many of whom belong to Equity as well as the NUJ.)

This is probably the best point to describe briefly some of the courses available to students with their eyes firmly fixed on a broadcasting career. Some, like the National Film and Television School and Ravensbourne College, have close links with bodies like the ITV Association, others do not have those direct links and there are many different emphases on the theoretical and practical thrust of particular courses. Many of them state that they are prepared to waive the entry requirements in individual cases, particularly for mature students with other experience instead, but otherwise there are varying fixed minimum criteria.

Bristol University runs a one-year course for postgraduates, with a first term 'crash course' to impart the minimum technical knowledge, and two terms in production of films and videos, fictional and documentary, on location and in the studio.

The Royal College of Art expects applicants to have a first degree and to submit up to 30 minutes of film or video demonstrating a high level of technical competence, supported where necessary with scripts or other material. It is a two-year course, the first of which is structured by the College, with lectures, seminars and exercises, and the final year is structured mostly by the student's own motivation. They are all expected to produce at least one major production, several of which have won prizes in film competitions in previous years.

Bournemouth and Poole College of Art and Design has also traditionally done well in the world of student film festivals. It offers a BTEC Higher National Diploma in photography, film and television. It is a two-year course offering an initial familiarisation followed by specialisation, with regular visits from practising professionals and a well-established industrial release programme. It is geared very much to the employment market.

The London International Film School has no specific entry qualifications, though in practice most of its students are graduates or possess the qualifications to go on to higher education. This is a two-year course in all aspects of film-making, theoretical and practical, in which each student takes in rotation each technical role from director to sound recordist, working in 16mm and 35mm, black-and-white and colour, sync and non-sync, and embracing all aspects of production — lighting, writing, editing, and budgeting. In the final term they must write a thesis or dissertation on a technical or aesthetic theme related to cinema.

The National Film and Television School also does not specify academic qualifications for entry, but encourages applications from talented individuals who should become 'well-rounded' specialists. Again all students get a basic grounding in all areas of film-making before concentrating on their own specialisation, and group activity is all-important. The course lasts for three years.

West Surrey College of Art and Design has a Department of Fine Art and Audio Visual Studies that embraces photography, film and video, and animation, with a three-year honours degree course. There are opportunities for a limited number of students to spend a period of up to 12 weeks of their course in an overseas college, normally during their second year of study, and also for students to spend short periods of time attached to commercial studios and production units of various kinds. Students are expected to participate in public exhibitions or screenings, and WSCAD has an enviable record in winning awards at national and international competitions and festivals. The course is one of those accredited by the ACTT, so graduating students gain an ACTT ticket.

The courses at the Central London Polytechnic, London College of Printing, and West Surrey College of Art and Design are all undergraduate courses, so you would need either five GCSEs including two at A level, or four GCSEs with three at A level. Their particular focus or emphasis varies considerably, and you would need to study each prospectus carefully to choose the one best suited to your own aptitude or interests. But what all three of these institutions have in common is that, although theory is not neglected, the main thrust of the courses is practically-based, and their expressed intention of relating the teaching to the needs of the industry means that the employment prospects of successful students are high.

In addition to these and other courses at universities, poly-technics, and colleges of art and design there is one other special course worth mentioning at this stage, Jobfit, which leads not to a degree or a diploma, but to something just as coveted in this business, and often harder to win — the ACTT ticket.

Jobfit was set up in 1985 by the ACTT, the Independent Programme Producers Association (IPPA), and the British Film and Television Producers Association (BFTPA), to train students specifically in the technical and production grades of film-making covered by the ACTT. It is not designed to train producers, directors or scriptwriters. Like most new schemes of entry Jobfit attracted a flood of initial applicants — more than 3000. The first dozen students started the two-year course in 1986, and the numbers admitted each year since then have increased. Entry is designed to open up the industry to a broader spectrum of people beginning in the junior technician grades. No formal qualifications are required, but the successful applicants must be able to demonstrate a commitment to film and film-making. It is very much an equal opportunities scheme and out of the 41 students in 1988 half were women and a third from ethnic minority backgrounds. The training follows an apprenticeship style of block release, beginning with a six-week introductory course at the Central London Polytechnic, the National Film

School, or West Surrey College of Art and Design. Trainees are then sent on a series of placements, based on their CVs and interviews. In the first year they are expected to experience working in a broad range of different grades and only to specialise in their second year. The off-the-job formal technical training continues at intervals in blocks of three or four weeks at a time.

There is continuous assessment with no formal examinations, and after the two years are up if they have successfully completed the course the Jobfit trainees join the freelance market with their ACTT ticket in their pocket and very likely a job with one of their placement employers.

So far I have described in mostly general terms the various methods of entry to the industry as a whole. But the world of broadcasting is made up of many specialist areas working on their own or in collaboration with other specialists, and I want to look at some of their needs next.

Profile Vision Mixer

Julie Miller joined TVS straight from college in 1987 at the age of 21. She was educated at Archer's Court Secondary School at Whitfield, near Dover, and was first attracted to a career in television when she attended a video course in Dover for schools and colleges on a day-release basis. Her other interests in photography, artwork and painting helped to gain her a place at Ravensbourne College, where she did the two-year television programme operations course. Part of the course was a six-week attachment observing operations at a TV station, and since her home was in that region she chose TVS. This confirmed her in her choice of career.

In her second year at college she did both vision-mixing and editing, but decided her temperament and interests were better suited to the former. She was encouraged to apply for an advertised vacancy at TVS where the Board consisted of the two Senior Vision Mixers, and Personnel. It was the latter who asked her the most technical question: 'What are the faults of the Grass Valley Mixer?' Since it was so much more impressive than any of the simpler ones she had ever operated she was stuck for an answer until the Head of Vision Mixers said she didn't know any faults in it either. She was more concerned to establish that Julie's preference really was for vision-mixing rather than editing.

She was appointed before she had finished her HND at College, so was advised to return to complete it — on her new TVS salary.

Her advice to applicants is to try and observe the operation as much as possible beforehand, to take any visual course but concentrate on choosing the right college. You need to have an eye for picture composition and a good ear for music. She had the advantage of being able to read music and plays the piano, violin and clarinet, so when she joined she did not need to be sent on the score-reading course. But the most important quality is probably the right temperament, you will always be under pressure in the gallery, and asked for split-second reactions on either live or recorded shows.

Her technical background at college reduced Julie's training period from nine months to six. To begin with she observed and marked-up scripts, and then operated under supervision. She only did parts of the live evening news magazine at first, and it was a little while before she mastered the complications of the weather forecast. She graduated from simple shows to more demanding ones and by her third year was expected to do everything, though when we talked she had yet to do her first game show, a genre which is deliberately cut very fast. She looks forward to doing everything in the field, including opera and other big music programmes, and cannot conceive of any other career she would enjoy so much.

3

Design

The breakneck advance of technology in the world of television design in recent years has made it one of the fastest-changing areas in television as far as recruitment and training are concerned. The rapid growth of facilities houses and independents outside the BBC and the ITV companies has led to probably the highest turnover of staff to be found anywhere in the business — up to 40 per cent or more a year in some cases. This has produced a situation where prospective employers come in search of the best talent rather than waiting to receive their applications. It is fairly common practice for Heads of Design departments in ITV and the BBC to do the rounds of the degree shows at colleges of art with contracts in their pockets to snap up the outstanding candidates before their competitors do. The various disciplines fall into two main divisions — scenic design and graphic design, with various sub-groups within them.

SCENIC DESIGN

It is essential to have a formal college of art training in interior design, sculpture, fine art, fashion, architecture, stage design or related disciplines, preferably up to BA level. Draughting skills are all important and candidates are judged on their portfolios. If some examples have already caught the eye of a prospective employer at the degree show you would still be invited to bring along a portfolio of work to the interview. This and your CV should, of course, be beautifully presented.

The normal point of entry is as a Scenic Design Assistant; after two years you might expect to advance to Senior Scenic Design Assistant, the big jump is then to Designer, where you would expect to have sole responsibility for designing major dramas or entertainment shows or other important programmes.

There is then at least a two-year progression to Senior Scenic Designer (these are the job-titles in ITV, the names are slightly different in the BBC, but the career progression is the same.)

Do not despair if you do not succeed in gaining entry at your first attempt. In design as in other parts of broadcasting varied experience is highly valued, and more than one attempt to join even the same company can be rewarded for persistence. However nervous you may be at your first interview try to listen carefully to any advice to prove you heard it second time around — but take a different folder of work that you have done in the intervening 12 months or whatever period has elapsed. The Head of Creative Services at one ITV Company told me that his current best designer had only been accepted at the third attempt.

Find out as much as you can about the job and the company before the interview. You may only have 20 minutes to change the course of your life, do not waste half of it finding out what the job entails. The interviewers will be seeking to find out about not just your experience and skills, but the breadth of your interests and knowledge of three dimensional design, contemporary and period furniture and architecture, fashion trends, theatre, television, and films.

Personality and the ability to express yourself are very important. Don't worry about any disagreements at the interview, but do be prepared to say why you disagree in a positive way. On the other hand it is not a good idea to criticise everything produced by your prospective employers, or they may wonder why you want to join them at all. They will be trying to assess how you would fit into a team. You will have to be able to convey your ideas verbally as well as visually to producers and directors and a variety of technicians who will have to realise your plans and carry them out to very precise specifications. This could be anything from a costume drama to a quiz-show, a light entertainment spectacular to an educational science programme, or a general election set to a Christmas music show — the starting-point for any of these could be an idea, a specific period or event, or just the number of people on set at various visual display points. Because any designer in the course of a year may be called on to work on perhaps an even wider range of programmes than the ones just mentioned, he or she must have as wide-ranging a background knowledge as possible.

Some designers manage to combine a successful career in

television whilst continuing their work as painters, or sculptors. Some move into direction (Ridley Scott was a designer who was sent on the same BBC directors' course as me in 1965, who went on to become a director first in BBC Television, then as a maker of commercials, to his present career as a highly-successful feature film director in the cinema).

There is also a certain amount of sideways movement between scenic design and graphic design, though this is most likely to happen early on in the individual's career because the initial skills and visual flair required may be helpful in either, but the specific technical knowledge varies considerably as you progress up the ladder.

GRAPHIC DESIGN

Recruitment here is generally from first degree level or equivalent diploma (usually a BTEC Higher), or postgraduate. In ITV this may be for a position on the staff, with a three month probationary period. In the BBC graphic design assistants may be recruited directly to staff posts but are more frequently offered short temporary contracts in the first instance, with subsequent interview boards being advertised internally. The effect is virtually the same for the aspiring graphic designer — he or she has to prove their worth in the first three months. John Aston, Graphic Design Manager at the BBC says 'I want people to compete from the moment they put their foot in the door.'

He visits all the London degree shows, and many colleges outside London now make a point of bringing their shows to London. Brighton Polytechnic has exhibited at Centrepoint, West Surrey College of Art and Design held a screening of animation work at the TVS London office, others have come to as varied settings as London Zoo or Capital Radio. It is very important to have a feel for typography — until recent years, an area where student interest had been rather low. The growth of computer-generated graphics seems to have raised the level of interest, but it is still necessary to have a good period knowledge of letter-form. The adaptation of that knowledge, when the logos of programmes like *Panorama* or *The News* or *Top of the Pops* are being incorporated into the studio set and graphics for the programme, means that lateral, not literal, thinking is wanted.

John Aston says that he is looking for 'well-educated people, who will be working with dramatists and composers (often producers allow graphic designers that freedom). Science producers will want someone with at least an interest in science, LE producers expect them to go to variety shows, and they would have to be able to appreciate Henry James, say, if it's a dramatisation of one of his novels.'

They have to possess obvious graphic designer potential and be able to draw exceedingly well. 'Drawing for the designer can be compared in influence to the samurai sword, since it leaves your opponent precisely where you want him, astounded and listening to your point of view.'

Graphic designers must be fully conversant with all forms of film, video and computer graphic technology, as well as the more conventional preparation methods for print, photography, illustration, typography and animation projects. But, as in the scenic design area, originality of ideas and treatment is at a premium, coupled with the ability to analyse information, distil it and communicate it in appropriate visual form.

BBC News and Current Affairs has around 70 design staff and there are nearly as many again in the other main programme areas. About seven or eight people a year are recruited for the latter, while News and Current Affairs needs about 30 new people a year. The speed and immediacy needed on these mostly live programmes means that keyboard skills for the caption generators are most in demand, supported by a BTEC National and a temperament that enjoys the cut and thrust of live television. New entrants are sent on a two-week training course at Evesham — the 'engineering familiarisation course' for young designers.

The arrival in rapid succession of new electronic systems such as Quantel, Artfile, Paintbox and Harry means a constant updating of the technical knowledge required to operate them, and the trained and experienced staff in the BBC and ITV are much sought-after in the rest of the industry. In 1988 a middle-size company like TVS had to recruit nine new BTEC graduates, and the launch of SKY Television in the same year caused a major exodus from BBC News and Current Affairs Graphics Department. Junior graphics staff gravitate towards the independents, the facilities houses, and the production companies who are buying operational skills. Senior staff with design and computing talent and producer expertise have tended to set up their own companies. Some are particular specialists as moving image graphic designers, like English Markell Pockett. But success in this competitive field is founded on some years of experience in ITV or the BBC and there is still no substitute for that kind of training.

Saul Bass, the famous American designer of film title credits who has been a great influence on generations of art students, was once asked at a public lecture the secret of his creative success. He replied 'I guess over the years I've developed some bigger muscles, but on the other hand I guess I'm handling heavier rocks.'

As you climb the ladder from Graphic Design Assistant to Graphic Designer and Senior Graphic Designer you too will be expected to develop bigger creative muscles across a very wide spectrum of programmes. John Aston believes that the best kind of client, ie producer, will identify the problem not the solution. The latter is up to the designer, who must always remember that he or she is working in the TV production business, not the graphic design business. The best graphics work is 'invisible', because it is there only to serve the needs of the programme, not to draw attention to itself and distract from the programme. His final word of advice is: 'The aspiring applicant would do well to remember that talent alone is never enough. There is a need too for application, wit and an ability to survive.'

WARDROBE

The first rung of the recruitment ladder is at the Wardrobe Assistant/Dresser level, where you would need O levels in English, history, art, mathematics and dressmaking, and probably experience in a theatre or film wardrobe department or at a theatrical custumiers. To progress up the ladder to Wardrobe Mistress/Master and then Senior Wardrobe Mistress/Master you would need to have attended an art college course in fashion or theatre design, or have done an apprenticeship in tailoring.

You would be working with artistes up to and during performance, at times of maximum tension for them, so a sensitive temperament is essential. Even the most experienced artistes are under stress, and younger or less experienced ones might be terrified, so you would need to know how much or when to talk to them and, above all, to always keep calm yourself.

Profile **Graphics Designer**

Mark Jefferson joined TVS at the age of 21. He was educated at St George's Church of England School in Gravesend, and Medway College of Art (now the Kent Institute of Art and Design), where he took a diploma and HND in graphics. He worked for a design firm in Rochester in his vacations, and also for about six months of his final year. When TVS wrote to the College suggesting that a number of students should come to the studios he was not selected by the lecturer, but went anyway. He spent a whole morning there viewing the electronic graphics in use and showing his portfolio.

A month later he was called for a second interview with six people on the Board. He prepared intensively for this with a totally new portfolio of work and stayed up the whole night beforehand putting the finishing touches to it, with only half an hour's sleep. Advised to take only about 15 items he in fact took 35, and is convinced that it was the quality of his work that got him the job. His advice to applicants is to spend a lot of money on a professional-looking portfolio and only put the very best in it, both colour and black-and-white. You need to have a good design sense, to take a TV course at college, and you must have the right personality to fit in with a team. Here too it is essential to be able to work under pressure of deadlines, often on the same day.

The competition is fierce — Mark was one of eight successful applicants out of a field of over 200. On joining he spent the first week on familiarisation with the facilities at the Maidstone studios, then four weeks intensive training at Southampton on the Aston III, Artfile, and at Logica in London for the Gallery 2000. He returned to his base at Maidstone working initially under supervision on the evening news magazine and other live shows. He was soon operating the Aston III on his own; it took longer to learn the Paint system, but he grabbed whatever time he could to master the intricacies of Paintbox, since the only way to learn it is to do it.

He would now hate to go back to print-graphics work, and loves the buzz that accompanies television programmes. He sees the next challenge as the multi-skills required on the new generation of graphics machines and is itching to get into that field, as well as title-sequence techniques. He is impressed by the sheer speed of operation in the leaders in his field, and thinks he may well eventually wish to go independent himself, but for the moment is content with the main ambition he expressed at his Final Board — to be Head of Graphics.

Period costumes are usually hired, which involves fittings and alterations, and often last-minute repairs, so sewing skills are essential. At more senior levels staff are involved in researching costume styles and authentic fabrics, and ensuring that colours and tones will blend with the set designs and meet the director's intentions. Unlike the theatre, every little detail will show in close-up, and the slightest mistake will immediately be picked up by keen-eyed and expert viewers.

The constant care of costumes, particularly on a long shooting-schedule in the studio or on location, means many hours working after the cast have finished for the day, for the necessary washing, cleaning or pressing.

Much television work is of course in contemporary dress, and it is just as important that presenters of news, informational and educational programmes should look appropriately dressed for their programmes. Wardrobe supervisors therefore frequently accompany artistes shopping for clothes to wear on-screen. Some patterns and colours have a most unfortunate effect on the camera lens, causing 'strobing' or 'picture noise'. (I once heard an American producer yell at a reporter who suddenly appeared on-camera wearing a jacket with a spectacularly large check pattern 'Tom, that jacket's the first I've seen with its own natural sound!')

The best training for this side of television work is backstage in a busy theatre where the pressure, excitement, and long, unsociable hours will prove an admirable preparation for a department that sometimes feels itself the Cinderella of design, constantly preparing everyone else for the ball. But for those with the right temperament and love for the job, it gives great satisfaction for both its constantly changing nature and its working relationship with performers and crew.

MAKE-UP

This is often bracketed together with wardrobe and the two are necessarily located together, since they are both working with artistes at almost the same time, and are in constant attendance during shooting.

Trainee Make-Up Artists should have a City and Guilds, DATEC or other recognised qualification in make–up and/or hairdressing, and/or beauty therapy, or an art school training in portraiture, sculpture or fine art. Some may have trained

1. *Television Sound desk during rehearsal (TVS)*

2. *Disc-Jockey Dave Austin on-air (BBC Radio Kent)*

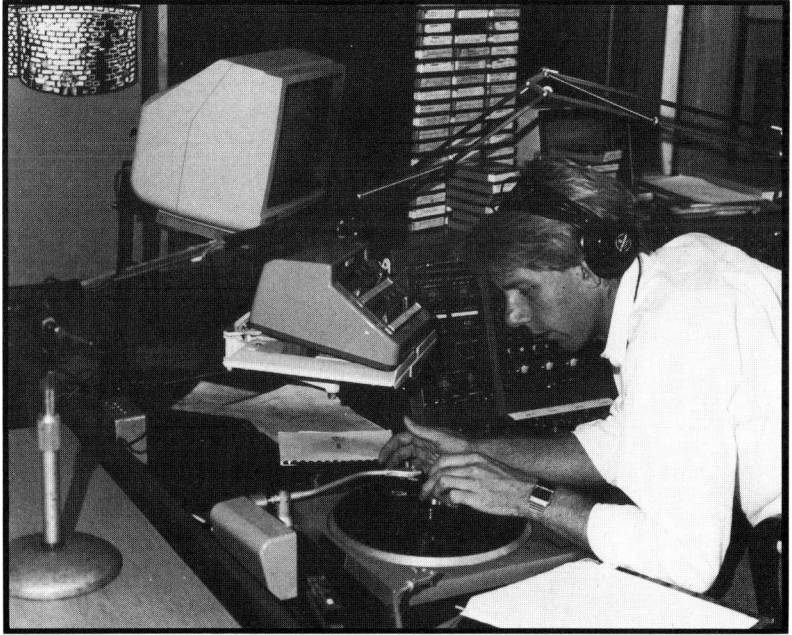

3. *Control-Room for Television News at Abingdon (Central Independent Television)*

4. *Location shooting for* THE SECRET LIFE OF ADRIAN MOLE *(Thames Television)*

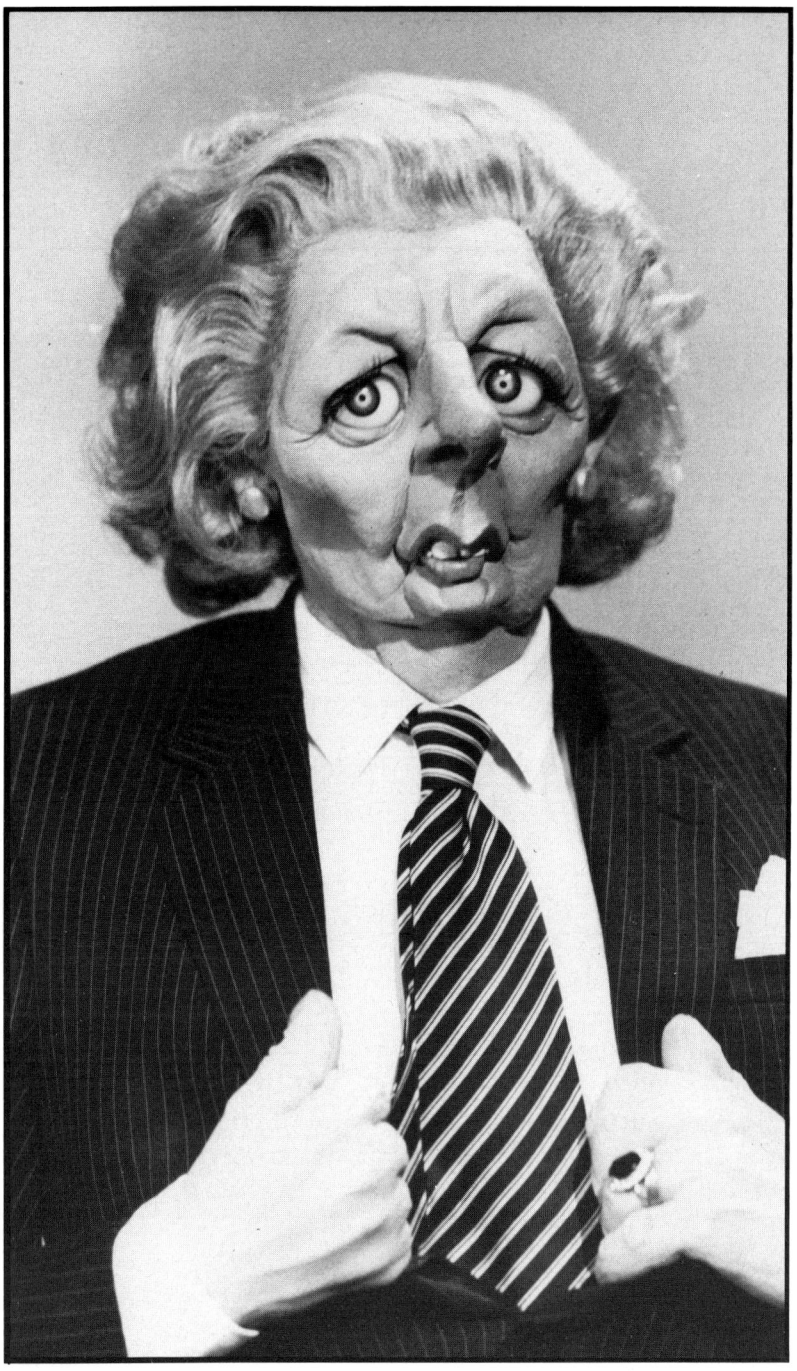

5. The SPITTING IMAGE of Mrs Thatcher (Central Independent Television/ Spitting Image Productions)

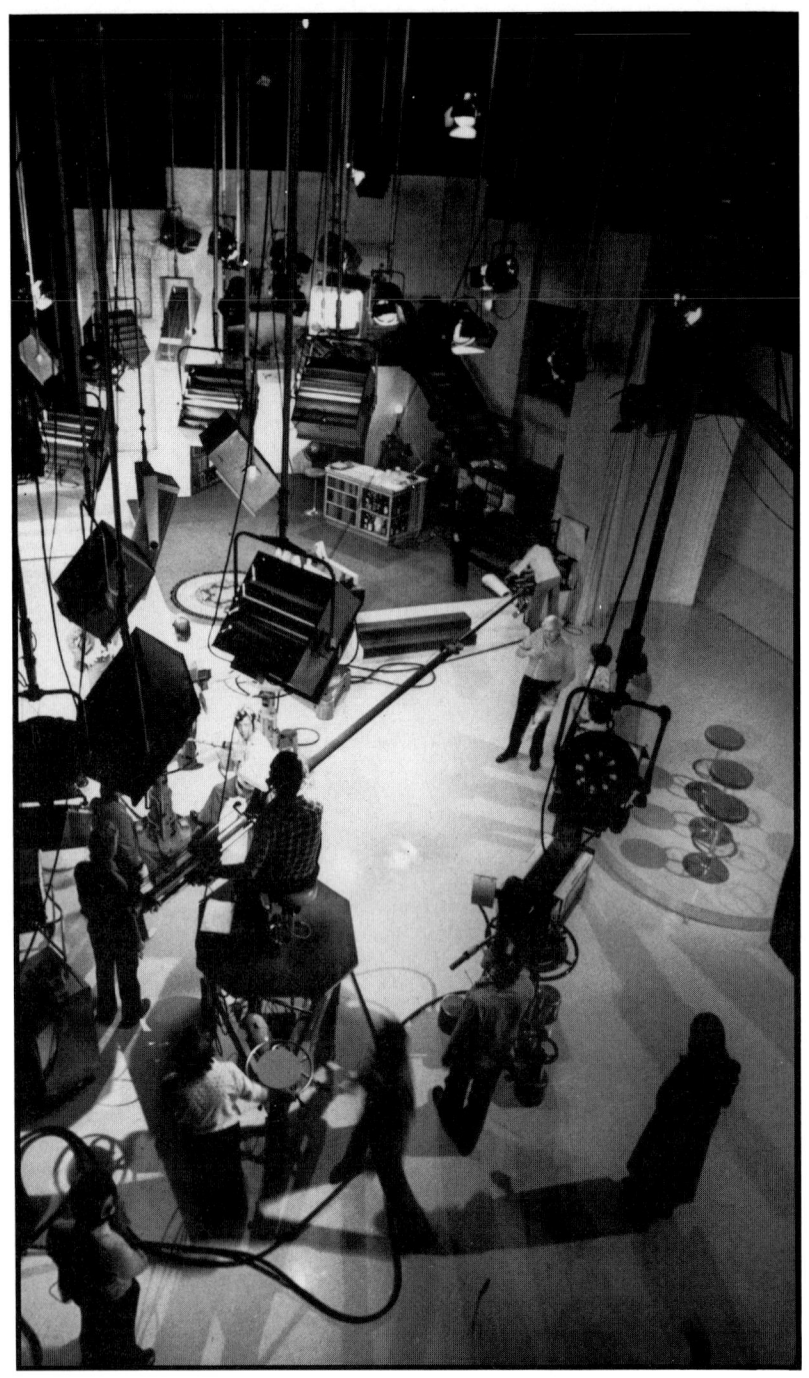

6. *Television Studio floor in rehearsal (Thames Television)*

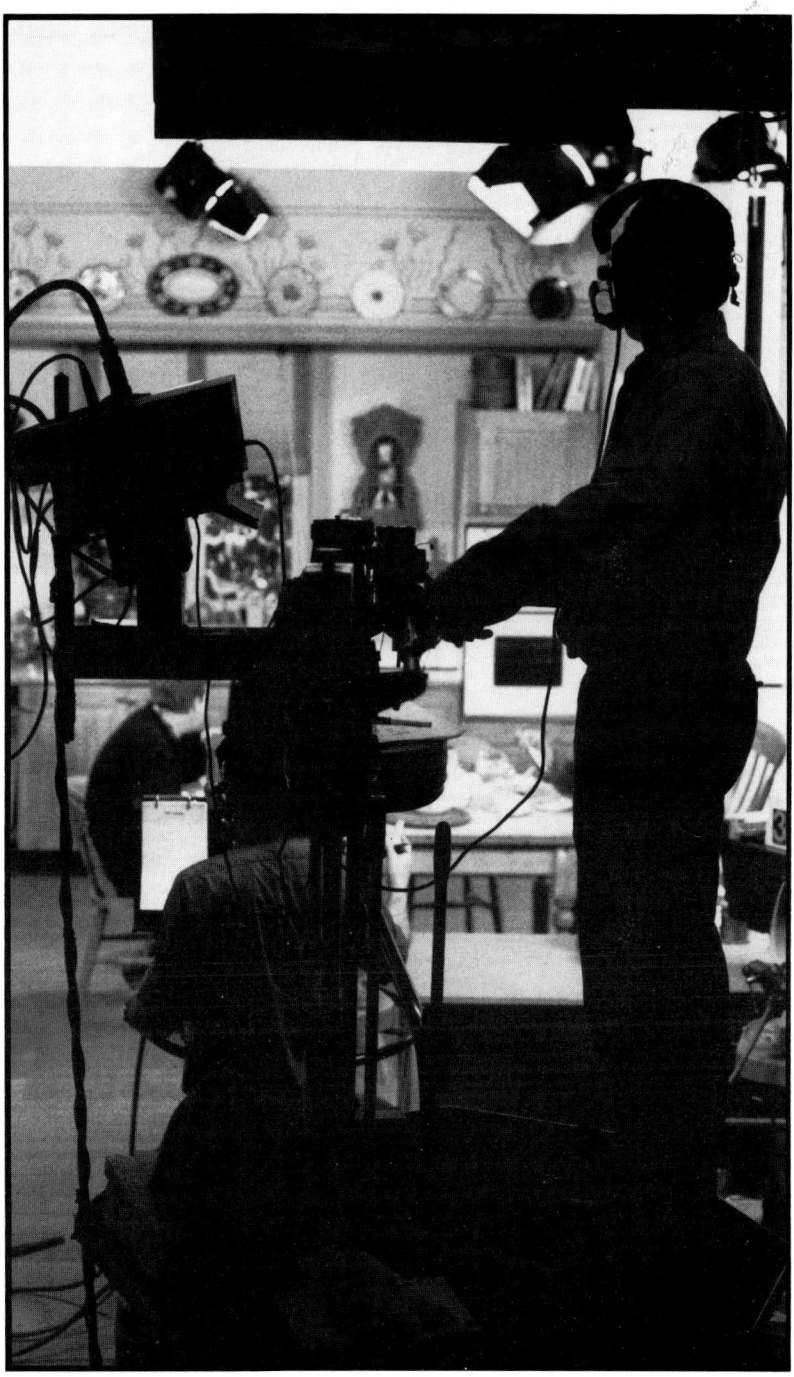

7. *Sound Boom-Operator in Television Studio (TVS)*

8. *BLUE PETER in rehearsal (BBC Children's Television)*

9. *The author (L) on location with Jill Cochrane and Denis Healey for A FULL LIFE (TVS)*

10. *TV Control-Room R to L Writer, P.A., Director Vision Mixer (TVS)*

11. *Lighting Control-Room. Lighting Director nearest camera (TVS)*

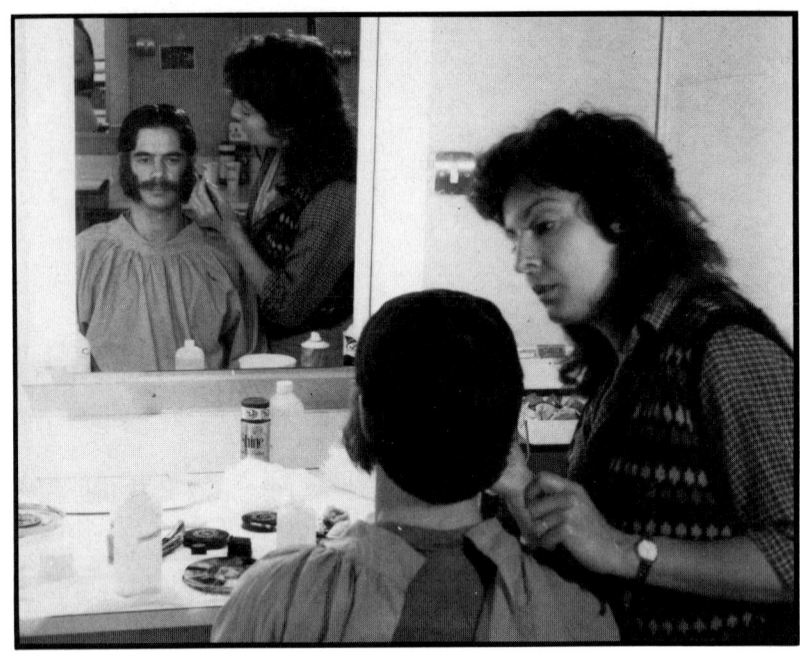

12. *Make-Up Department (BBC Open University)*

13. *Electronic Graphics – The Quantel Paintbox (BBC Open University)*

with one of the large cosmetic houses as a beautician working in a large store.

Here too some experience of the kind of backstage frenzy found in the world of the theatre is useful, since Make-Up Artists need to possess the same calming temperament as their colleagues in Wardrobe, only even more so; they will spend rather more of their time working with non-professional contributors who may well have never been on television before, as well as politicians or other public figures under pressure, who may be tired, apprehensive, or even angry about the issues they have come in to discuss. The Make-Up Artist is frequently the last person they meet before making their appearance, so could bear the brunt of their nervous tension to which the only response must be a sweet smile. Great tact can be needed with some people over a certain age, who might be self-conscious or even secretive about a wig or a toupee. (I have seen Denis Healey joking while his famous eyebrows are brushed, but many senior female politicians will usually demand much more time in make–up than his five minutes in the chair, and refuse to leave it to start the programme until they are happy with their appearance.)

Presence of mind in a crisis can even get you the job. One candidate on her way to an interview at TVS had the misfortune of her car breaking down on the M27. She rang the studios to explain even before she rang the AA, finally turned up for the Board two hours late only slightly flustered, and got the job.

For obvious reasons make–up in television is a job customarily performed by women (though oddly enough in the cinema most make–up artists are men), and although in these days of equal opportunities legislation vacancies will be open to both sexes it is likely that make–up will remain an almost exclusively female preserve for the foreseeable future.

4

Television programme departments

The qualities and aptitudes required to enter the field of television production in general are by now probably fairly apparent, but different departments often look for radically different skills. The person most suited for an educational department for example is unlikely to succeed in light entertainment and vice versa, at least initially — there are some notably successful cases of people switching horses in mid-career from, say, sport to politics, schools to music and arts, or science to drama. But for most people, their first appointment is likely to shape the whole of their subsequent career. So it is important to know in your own mind which area appeals to you most.

LIGHT ENTERTAINMENT

If you want to make programmes for some of the biggest audiences in television this is where you should aim. The BBC and the ITV companies are perpetually locked in combat for audiences in peak-time with situation comedies and variety shows, pop music, quizzes, game shows and chat shows, and frequently they are in competition for the services of the big stars. Morecambe and Wise switched channels several times, an example followed by such names as Michael Parkinson and Clive James, who moved in opposite directions.

The Head of the Light Entertainment Group in the BBC, Jim Moir, says he is looking for entrants 'with fire in their belly, a sense of vocation, with a wish to excel and make a contribution'. Many of them will have 'got up on the boards' themselves — an understanding of performance skills is crucial in this area. They will have often demonstrated initiative and organisational skills; one recent entrant had been the Entertainments Officer at Middlesex Polytechnic, where he had set up a group of other Polytechnics to book shows for them all.

Jim Moir is looking for three particular qualities:

1 — ' A director of the written word, who can direct a script, shape a script, even perform a script.'

2 — 'The ability to direct an artiste, and a performance, and draw out the performance of a script.'

3 — 'The ability to direct cameras to bring out the performance and enhance the script and/or the performance.'

He says most trainees fail on number 1. The sum of what he is seeking in the successful applicant is 'a creative contribution to the editorial content, an ability to grasp all the elements and enhance them. The grammar of TV can be learnt, judgement can be refined and improved by practice, but they must have an innate understanding of what the prime duty is and the flair to present it in a way that makes the audience find it compelling, ie funny.'

Frank Muir used to joke when he lectured BBC training courses in the '60s about a Head of Comedy with no sense of humour (and hinted he was only half-joking!), but you would certainly not get far in Jim Moir's Department without a highly-developed one.

His own career path is quite an instructive one. He read history at Nottingham University, where I spotted his gift for making people laugh and gave him his first stage part as Baudricourt's Steward in *St Joan*. He applied for one of the new BBC–2 Traineeships at the end of 1963. He was sent immediately on the six-week Directors' Course and then to the Light Entertainment Department as Production Manager trainee to David Croft, a producer with a long list of LE credits to his name. After six months he was made Production Manager, a position he held for the next seven years, working on the whole range of output, from *Top of the Pops*, *Juke Box Jury* and *Dee Time* to *A Degree of Frost* and *The Benny Hill Show*. This involved working with the director and cast in rehearsal rooms and then on the studio floor as the director's intermediary from the gallery control-room to the performers. (He was once rebuked by one famous comic for making the crew laugh with his own jokes — 'I make the funnies round here!')

After that long apprenticeship he became first an Assistant Producer and then quite quickly a full Producer in 1970. In

11 years as a Producer he tended to specialise in comedy and variety shows, including *The Generation Game* which he piloted. He became an Executive Producer in 1980, and Head of Variety in 1982, a position he retained when he was promoted to Head of Light Entertainment Group.

New entrants to his Group can be counted on both hands, with the number fluctuating between about six and ten each year. They are mostly under 30, usually around 25, and about a third of all these Trainee Production Managers are female. Most of them apply directly to the LE Group, but since 1988 the Group has also been represented on the Appointments Boards for Production Trainees to help spot suitable people. Jim Moir also emphasises the importance of what he calls 'banana entry via radio, coming in sideways.'

With understandable pride he claims that BBC Light Entertainment is the greatest missionary society in broadcasting: 'All the stars of ITV LE like Jimmy Gilbert (Thames), Marcus Plantin (LWT), Duncan Wood (Yorkshire), and Alan Boyd (TVS), are ex BBC. You need a critical mass-weight of product for the passing on of skills, and a large enough pool of excellence to which people can aspire. It doesn't guarantee success, but it inhibits error.'

In ITV most of the LE production teams tend to be freelance, brought in on short-term contracts for particular shows or series. In practice these can often roll on if a particular show is a success — *The Benny Hill Show* ran for years, and *Blind Date*, *Give us a Clue*, and *Bobby Davro* could also be set for long runs. But comedy is such an unpredictable commodity that hits seem to be fewer than the misses. The biggest shortage is not the performers but the writers, and this is one important reason why situation comedies are far outnumbered by game shows and chat shows which do not have that absolute dependence on the scriptwriter. To succeed in this area you need to be buzzing with ideas that will appeal to a mass audience.

CHILDREN'S

In adult programme departments producers will have been accused at one time or another of making programmes for themselves rather than the audience, but in children's television you can only succeed if you really want to make programmes for this audience, which stretches from preschool into the teens, from *Jackanory* to *Grange Hill*. The commitment to the audience is often so great that some people spend their entire career happily working in this area, reaching two or maybe even three generations of the same family.

Within both ITV and the BBC the people in charge of the programmes tend to be mature with a lot of experience of both television and the audience, but the production offices are noticeably full of very active young people in their early or mid twenties. ITV frequently advertises for direct entry from outside, and work with children's theatre or other close contact with the audience is a useful qualification.

In the BBC currently much of the recruitment to this department is internally through the BBC Attachment Scheme, numbering about six Assistant Production Trainees a year. These have come from such areas as Presentation, Assistant Film Editors, Floor Managers or Assistant Floor Managers, and secretaries (an exception to my warning in Chapter 1). Hospital radio or local radio experience is valuable for both external and internal applicants. 'Equal opportunity' means precisely that here — the staffing ratios are almost exactly 50-50 for men and women.

Anna Home is Head of Children's Television and her career path is also instructive. She entered the BBC as a graduate Studio Manager recruit, initially working at Broadcasting House, then spent three years at Bush House in the External Services. She applied for one of the BBC–2 Traineeships but was turned down. She then became a researcher in Children's TV and her first programme was *Playschool*. She never went on the BBC Directors' Course but learnt to direct on the job. As *Jackanory* evolved out of *Playschool* Anna became first a director then a producer (here the rough division is between someone responsible for directing cameras and primarily concerned with pictures, and someone primarily concerned with the theme and the word). She persuaded the then Head of the Department, Monica Sims, into a commitment to children's drama, and one of the first was a six-part film serial shot entirely on location in Newcastle, entitled *Jo and the Gladiator*. From 1975 to 1981 she was Executive Producer for Children's Drama, and was responsible for starting *Grange Hill*, which was successful with its young target audience but controversial with older viewers and parents because of its realism and strong language. She was a founder-promoter of TVS and established it as a major provider of children's programming to the ITV Network. In 1986 she returned to the BBC to head the Department she had first joined in television as a researcher.

As you might expect from someone with such a depth of experience in this field she has a great interest in and knowledge of children's literature, and has very little time for people who only see her department as a stepping-stone to what they think are higher things: 'Anyone who hasn't done their homework, and looked at the output, should be shot!'

By its very nature children's television is seen by few adults apart from eavesdropping parents, and very few other people working elsewhere in the business, so there is an occasional tendency to feel forgotten and unappreciated. To more than compensate, the target audience is probably the most enthusiastic and loyal of any segment of the population. Viewer correspondence regularly runs into thousands, whereas even the most hotly controversial adult documentary feels flattered if its mail reaches three figures or more.

DRAMA

Here commitment is all important, since the hurdles to entry into television drama seem to be many, and high. In the first place this has become almost entirely a field for the freelance on short-term contract, and secondly the entry point is rather later than for most other departments. There is a clear division of roles in drama, between directors and producers. (Because of the scale and complexity of the tasks involved it is very rare now for one person to combine the two functions.)

In the early days of ITV it was quite common to have a small number of staff directors, notably in what was then ATV, echoing the similar BBC practice. By the early '70s these numbers had contracted to the point of disappearance, so if you want the security of a staff position you can forget about a career in television drama now. (There are still a few staff producers in the BBC, but I will come to producers in a moment.)

Theatre experience is essential: in the '50s and '60s the BBC policy was a minimum of three years' experience. This was most often to be found in the provincial repertory companies, but since their numbers are now somewhat diminished alternative experience can be gained in the world of film. Whereas previously university graduates managed occasionally to go straight into television drama, now new entrants are more likely to be found coming from the film schools. More drama is being made on film, encouraged by the long-running rival strands, *Screen Two* and *Film on Four*. The great training ground traditionally has been the twice-weekly soap operas, where many now well-known names first cut their teeth and learnt the technical side of the business coping with that relentless conveyor belt. Michael Apted is but one name among many television and feature-film directors who owe much to being blooded on *Coronation Street* at the outset of their directorial careers.

Coronation Street is now one of the few such series still to be shot in the studio. Many of the others, such as *Brookside* or *Eastenders*, are now shot on location. The new lightweight electronic cameras mean that location shooting can be either on tape or film, and the once common distinction between studio and film directors is now a thing of the past. To be considered a really top-class director today you have to be good on film. The economics of ambitious drama series or serials, or even single plays, has increasingly taken drama into the world of international co-production, for which the commonly acceptable medium is film rather than videotape.

Equal opportunity has lagged a bit in this area. There are a few more women directors than there were, but they are still outnumbered by the men by about nine to one. The entry point is around the age of 30 — a result of gaining that necessary experience in the world of drama outside television. Many come in as Production Managers working to experienced television directors before they get their first chance to direct, which in the BBC would probably only come after they had been on the Directors' Course. This longer apprenticeship has the compensation that the successful directors can, and do, go on into their sixties and occasionally even their seventies.

Producers have grown in importance in recent years. They have always had a major say in the choice of writer and shaping of the script, but nowadays that influence encompasses choosing the cast and locations, and administering the whole shooting and editing schedule, and above all the budget. This frees the director to concentrate on the creative realisation of the script. Naturally there has to be a close and mutually trusting relationship and the divisions will not always be as clear-cut as that, depending on the nature of the two people concerned, or maybe three if there are many episodes. It is no accident that the same team of producer and director can be seen working in tandem again and again for different companies on different shows — the relationship can be difficult to forge, and once forged is not lightly dropped for others that may be less fruitful.

Graham Benson, Controller of Drama at TVS, is one who worked his way up through the producer ranks from various provincial repertory theatres to the BBC as Production Manager and then Producer. Following that he went to Euston Films, the Robert Stigwood Group (an international production house), and then formed his own independent company where he was among those who worked out the operational brief for commissioning Independents by Channel 4. He was then Producer or Executive Producer at a number of ITV companies, at Consolidated Productions, and then back to the BBC, before joining TVS in 1986.

His credo has always been 'Don't stifle people's creative freedom'. He believes that even in the uncertainties of television in the '90s there will always be a place for drama. 'We are a story telling and story reading nation, there will always be a huge appetite for drama.' He is concerned that new writing may be at risk because of competitive pressure, but is trying to counter this by spending a longer time on script development — sometimes up to a year — before going into production.

Conscious from his own experience how hard it is to break into this side of the business he sees personally about 50 eager 20 to 21 year-olds a year to offer advice. His motto for them is 'Nil Desperandum. You have to stick at it if it's what you really want to do; you've got to be passionate about it and think it's the only thing you will do really well.'

Ronald Eyre put the same point to me years ago when I had just started in television and was torn between my two great interests in the theatre and the world of politics. He was then the Schools TV Drama Producer and about to embark on his freelance career in theatre and television. He told me then 'You should only devote your life to drama if you feel that it's the only way to make sense of your life.'

There are a number of people who can bear out the need for this single-minded determination to succeed in drama. One particular case that should appeal to those frustrated by the orthodox routes of entry is that of James Gatward.

Before National Service he worked in Rep as a small-part

actor and Assistant Stage Manager. When he was demobbed he answered an advertisement for motorcycle messengers at the BBC because he needed the money. He put his name down for TV stagehand and met Jack Good, producer of the pop show *Oh Boy*, who introduced him to ABC Television. Though James says he was the best stagehand at Teddington he applied for Boards as an Assistant Floor Manager to no avail. Having read of the opening of commercial TV in Canada he emigrated in 1959 with just £100 to his name. In Toronto he convinced Murray Chercover of CFTO that he was the best floor manager in England. In nine months he had became Master Control Director (what we call a Presentation Director). He moved to CFCF in Montreal when it opened in 1961, and directed everything in the studio, including the majority of 136 episodes of drama. Then he went freelance as a drama director for CBC in Toronto, for NBC in New York, and returned to the UK in 1965. Westward employed him to make investigative and dramatised documentaries, then he spent two years directing the drama series *The Troubleshooters* for the BBC. Asked to direct a Scottish historical series called *The Borderers* he shot it like a Western using many tricks he had learnt in America, and made a star out of the then unknown Michael Gambon.

By now he was sufficiently in demand by several ITV companies to set up his own production company in 1968, and made *Elephant Boy* as the first fully independent film drama series for the ITV Network and ABC — the beginning of many collaborations with Australia. To cut costs on the foreign location he bought the Land Rovers he needed direct from British Leyland in Britain and exported them to Sri Lanka, thus paying no tax on the vehicles and allowing him to sell them to the army when the shoot was finished. On another occasion he saved considerable sums on his budget by shooting on a demolition site at the right moment. This organisational flair became one of his greatest strengths. In 1977 he started to put together a group bidding for one of the ITV franchises and took a year off to work on it. He identified ATV, Southern and Westward as vulnerable to outside bids and eventually settled on Southern Television as his target; he had directed programmes there and knew the nature of the competition.

In between he continued to direct *Minder*, *The Misfit* and *East End Tales*; the latter all on a single electronic or film camera on location and in the studio, an early forerunner of what only became general practice elsewhere in the late Eighties.

His bid won the Southern franchise for TVS at the end of 1980 and his present position as Chief Executive has taken him a long way from hands-on direction. He has some regrets about that, and also about the changes he has seen in his zigzag career: 'When I came into TV it was so exciting. People had a lot of fun then, I don't see them doing that now.'

He fears it is more difficult now for young people to learn, since the old system of trailing experienced directors has largely disappeared. That vital work experience cannot be gained from the book or the classroom. His own managerial experience and entrepreneurial skills were honed by running his own company and coping with some difficult and occasionally hazardous shoots on foreign locations. When a man died in Sri Lanka during the *Elephant Boy* shoot James suddenly found himself arrested for murder and had some nasty moments before that misunderstanding was sorted out. After that kind of test, the stresses and strains of high finance and big co-productions do not seem so daunting.

The importance of James Gatward's story is not that he was lucky, but that he made his own luck. He took risks and bluffed his way into volatile situations. He survived because he had the talents and imagination to match his nerve. He also worked incredibly hard and taught himself the skills he lacked and knew he needed if he was not going to remain just another journeyman director.

What he believes, and so does everyone else in the particularly demanding world of drama, is that real talent will emerge if it is there, but only if it is allied with an all-consuming determination to make a mark. That means a willingness to do anything to learn, and not to mind starting at the very bottom.

You should also go to the cinema and theatre as often as you can, watch as wide a variety of television drama as possible, and simply observe with a voracious eye. Graham Benson says: 'You can't learn production behaviour, how to direct the actors, but you can learn the technical side — design, lighting, budgeting, script construction, film language.'

You will find it a struggle if you cannot learn the latter, you will find it impossible if you do not possess the former.

5

Educational broadcasting

The last three decades have seen a massive expansion of educational broadcasting in both production and consumption. ITV and BBC Schools Television began over 30 years ago with only a few hundred sets in schools, and by 1963 when I first started working in this area there was still some strong teacher resistance, and the number of schools taking the programmes was still only in the low thousands. Today nine out of 10 schools are regular users of the output, and many have not only several sets but audio-visual departments to record off-air and arrange the playbacks.

Further Education has steadily grown since the '60s, and its change of name to Continuing Education marked a recognition that many adults had, and have, an overpowering wish to expand both their knowledge and their critical faculties. Some of this need can be met informally through particular series, with or without the accompanying support materials; much more formally-structured instruction is provided by the Open University, and now the Open College.

The different providers of educational programmes decided long ago that, unlike their colleagues in most other departments, their channel schedules should not directly compete with each other. So there are various liaison committees where BBC, ITV and Channel 4 staff meet to discuss their respective future plans, to try and ensure that they are not scheduling the same kinds of programmes aimed at the same target audiences at the same time. The audience for, say, computer skills, health education, or series for the handicapped, would not appreciate it if two complementary series it wanted to see or hear were going out simultaneously for the same 10 weeks, and then nothing at all for the rest of the year. On occasions it has been discovered that two almost identical series have been planned quite independently and in ignorance of each other, and one has been dropped or postponed until a later time.

This is not to say that the competitive spirit is not present in the different wings of the educational broadcasting world. On the contrary, there is a healthy rivalry that contributes greatly to the quality of the service. There is certainly plenty of room for it. Adults can choose from over 4000 programmes a year transmitted across four channels — in an average week you can find between 50 and 60 hours of educational material.

What sort of people produce it, and what qualifications do you need to join them? You do not have to have teaching experience, though in practice quite a number do, particularly in the schools departments. You do not have to be a specialist in a particular discipline, though again the majority of schools producers are (and nearly everyone at the Open University, which I will deal with separately later, is a specialist). There are some highly successful producers without a degree, though these are in a small minority and have reached their position because of outstanding alternative knowledge and skills. It would be difficult to produce an adult language series without fluency in that particular foreign language, or a schools science or mathematics series without the appropriate degree. But an aptitude for communicating with the young, the handicapped, the illiterate or innumerate, the technically or historically minded, can equip you for work across a wide spectrum of programmes.

The pressures on airtime mean that you would, in any case, be expected to move across that spectrum as required. Recruitment is steady but not spectacular. In the BBC new entrants into Continuing Education and School Television number on average something between six and ten people per annum, with a male/female ratio of about 50:50. For the equivalent departments in Radio it has been about double that, with women outnumbering the men by about 3:1. Some of these were internally recruited from elsewhere in the BBC. Recent external advertisements produced some fluctuations in numbers — a researcher contract for School Television brought 40 applications, and one for Continuing Education brought 100, whereas in School Radio three producer vacancies attracted over 600 applicants from outside.

Eurfron Gwynne Jones, Controller of Educational Broadcasting at the BBC, says that most of these are graduates and usually already working in education, at school or higher education level. She looks for people who have demonstrated an interest in drama, concerts, the school newspaper, or taken other initiatives above and beyond their role in the school. It helps if they have already used educational broadcasting but certainly 'they must show some knowledge of the programme area'. By now this should not surprise you, since it is the constant refrain of everyone already quoted in this book. She also believes that in the rapidly changing world of broadcasting today staff should move out of education much more. This is much easier to do at assistant producer level than it is on the higher grades, but not impossible — John Prescott Thomas was a General Trainee who went on attachment to School Television, became an Assistant Producer, Producer, Senior Producer and then Head of Department there before going to BBC Bristol where, as Head of Broadcasting, South and West, he is now responsible for all that Region's output across radio and television. He says he never had a particular 'career plan' in mind, but originally opted for School Television because it covered such a wide variety of subjects and formats. He imagined it would be a good apprenticeship but stayed there for so long because he loved the work and the close contact with the audience.

This attitude is commonly found amongst school producers in both the BBC and ITV. Philip Grosset (Controller, Education and Religion at Central Television) believes that whereas adult education programmes can be successfully produced by non-specialists this is not true of programmes for schools — these must be produced by specialists who know the audience.

Before leaving the world of school television, it is worth underlining that the important disciplines required there — a clear narrative thread, good writing, logical development of ideas, only using the appropriate visual illustration — stand you in very good stead in other demanding areas. Some outstanding alumni of BBC School Television include Michael Gill (*Civilisation, America* and *Vintage*), Peter Montagnon (*The Long Search, Heart of the Dragon*), Colin Nears (*Joseph Conrad,Schubert* and *The Royal Ballet*), Ed Goldwyn (*Horizon*) and Andrew Neal (*The Living Planet*).

In Continuing Education some of the programmes are very clearly targeted, and in many instances are made in close collaboration with different agencies in the community — the Adult Literacy and Basic Skills Unit (ALBSU), the Health Education Authority (HEA), The Royal Society for Mentally Handicapped Children and Adults (MENCAP), and many others.

Other series will be watched by many people who will not

even be aware that they are educational programmes — cookery, keep-fit, various crafts, arts and history, the environment, all of these come within the ambit of education, though the line is blurred because other programmes on these subjects are also often made by non-educational departments.

The educational broadcasting map was largely redrawn with the arrival of Channel 4. The output of Naomi Sargant, the first Senior Commissioning Editor for Education, was soon seven and a half hours per week, 15 per cent of the Channel's output. In line with the Channel's overall policy about half was commissioned from the Independents and the other half from the ITV companies. For the most successful of the latter this was a major increase in production, though each series had to be negotiated separately with no guarantee of a commission. A number of educational producers from ITV and the BBC set up on their own as Independents to make programmes for Channel 4, with varying degrees of success. From 1987 Channel 4 also made its airtime available to take the ITV Schools transmissions; and the Open College broadcasts produced by ITV and Independents, commissioned directly by the Open College.

THE OPEN UNIVERSITY

The BBC Open University Production Centre is situated on the campus of the Open University at Milton Keynes, and its productions for the OU are funded out of the University's grant from the Department of Education and Science, not out of the BBC licence. It is a bi-media operation, producing around 160 television programmes and video-cassettes a year for the University, 360 radio programmes and audio-cassettes, and various other materials including interactive videodiscs and computer-synchronised audio. It also now produces about 40 videos a year for various outside agencies.

The full-time BBC staff required for this diverse operation (production, engineering, film and video operations, and design) numbers around 360. The latter three groups require the same qualifications as their fellows in the rest of the BBC, but the requirements for the 55 or so producers are rather more specialised. Not only do they need the usual professional broadcasting skills for educational production, but they must be academically qualified in the particular discipline in which they are working. There are now over 130 courses produced by seven faculties — Arts, Mathematics, Science, Social Science, Technology and the Schools of Education and Management. In addition the Continuing Education programme offers a range of single courses and diplomas in such areas as management education, computer applications, manufacturing methods and other professional topics.

There is not space here to describe the full complexity of the Open University partnership with the BBC. Suffice it to say that the BBC production staff are expected to play a full part in the course teams producing the course materials — printed as well as broadcast — and their credibility depends just as much on their academic knowledge as it does on their professional skills. This is why the great majority of the original production staff were recruited from university teaching and trained in the necessary broadcasting skills, working to a handful of experienced senior staff drawn largely from the other BBC education departments. Many of these original recruits have themselves now moved on within the BBC, or to ITV companies, Channel 4, or the Independent sector.

The nature of the producer/academic partnership was best described in principle by the Planning Committee in 1969:

'The success of this partnership rests on the recognition by both parties that, while effective education is the overriding objective, and the ultimate responsibility of the University under its charter, each has a specific professional role to play. The University will prescribe the audience objectives and general character of the broadcasts, in relation to the other component parts of each course, while the BBC will provide the necessary presentation and production skills. In the overlapping area — where the inter-relationship of content and presentation is worked out — a reasonable degree of flexibility on both sides is essential in order to secure the proper concern of the academic staff and the fullest use of the experience of the broadcasting staff. Within this area, such matters as the choice of principal academic contributors to programmes and the interconnection of subject instruction and broadcasting method will be of first importance to both partners. While the BBC recognises the right of the Open University finally to determine any such points that may be at issue, the University agrees that full participation of BBC staff in all discussion pertaining to these matters is a necessary condition of working effectively together. The key

relationship between contributors and production staff jointly engaged in producing material and programmes for broadcasting will thus be secured.'

In practice the success of that relationship hinges directly on the degree of mutual trust and respect between the individual BBC producer and the OU academic. The key words above are 'a reasonable degree of flexibility on both sides is essential.' As a general rule I found that the more distinguished and authoritative the academic (and I had the good fortune to work with a number of these), the greater their flexibility. But if you do not relish the intellectual cut and thrust of academic debate then the Open University is not the place for you.

The turnover of staff at Milton Keynes currently is about five per cent per annum for producers, and two or three times that for production assistants. John Radcliffe, Head of the Open University Production Centre from 1984-9, says: 'Our staff at OUPC need to be talented, tough minded, dedicated and skilled. They must be educators, knowing their fields well, with good instincts for communicating serious ideas. Their programmes have to capture the imagination of students whose time is precious, and help them to learn, otherwise they will be rejected. They must be good partners and teamworkers, not just in production but within the University. They need the vision and imagination to innovate, and the conviction and persuasiveness to win regard and respect and get their ideas across, in the OU and outside it. Above all, they need to be committed to the idea of quality, to the BBC's traditions of excellence in educational broadcasting, and to the Open University's historic mission of reaching out across Britain to open up higher education to those that missed their chance of it when they were younger.'

6

News and Current Affairs

THE BBC

Until recently there was a fairly rigid dividing line between News and Current Affairs departments, particularly in the BBC, but this has now largely disappeared even there, and staff move relatively freely between the news bulletins and the programmes of comment and analysis. In the BBC as a whole there are about 2000 people working in these departments in radio and television, in regional and national centres. Since the 1987 amalgamation into one Directorate of News and Current Affairs at the BBC, the television side has been divided for administrative convenience into the daily programmes — *Breakfast Time*, *The One O'Clock News*, *Six O'Clock News*, *Nine O'Clock News* and *Newsnight*, and the weekly programmes — *Panorama*, *Question Time*, *The Money Programme*, *On The Record* and others.

There is a further division into Intake, which can be described as the newsgathering side of the operation — the on-screen reporters and correspondents plus their production support staff — and Output, the staff who produce the programmes named above. The Intake side has a current strength of about 120 reporters and correspondents at home and abroad, supported by another 40 staff on the Foreign Desk, Home Desk, planners and field producers.

The daily output is maintained by approximately 200 staff, with rather fewer working on the weekly programmes, since their total transmission hours are less. The organisation of the production teams is the same for both. Each has a Programme Editor, with under him or her in descending levels of experience and responsibility various grades of Senior Producer, Producer, Assistant Producer, and Researcher. The joining level for new recruits is at the latter two grades.

There are various routes of entry:

1 — People with professional journalistic backgrounds. Most senior posts are in practice recruited internally, but others at Assistant Producer and Producer level are advertised externally. The relevant experience may have been gained in national, regional or local radio, provincial or national newspapers, or in television. There is a small sprinkling with existing television experience, but most come from the worlds of radio and the press. For some reason the regional television and radio centres have tended to provide fewer applicants than the local radio stations.

2 — The Broadcast Journalist Scheme, known in the BBC as 'the fast-track scheme', which identifies the potential high-fliers and puts them through an intensive training course including on-the-job training at a responsible level.

3 — The Broadcast Writers Scheme. This is recruited into at the Assistant Producer level, and these days it involves not just writing scripts for all the material coming in from BBC News Intake, agency and foreign sources, but putting the video packages together complete with all the necessary graphics.

The setting-up of more specialist units, the creation of new programmes, and the expansion of Parliamentary coverage means that News and Current Affairs (NCA) is presently expanding, so employment prospects here are improving. In addition there is some movement to features and documentary units inside the BBC and to other companies outside, including satellites and independents.

Within the NCA Directorate itself there are three main areas of career progression. New recruits who want to end up as on-screen reporters, have to go through intensive auditions and screen tests at the short-list stage, to see if they look and sound authoritative, as well as possessing the ability to research and write a story. As you might expect, this is one of the most competitive areas, with a constant flood of applicants. Chris Cramer, who is Managing Editor Intake, says he looks for a high degree of aggression. 'It is so competitive that there is no room for passengers on-screen in network television.'

Others will seek to achieve the editorial power of the programme editors, to decide with Intake which stories shall be covered, how and at what length. Others will be drawn to in-the-field production and film making (though in most cases today the medium is more likely to be video tape than celluloid);

from short reports for news they may graduate to a 15 minute report for *Newsnight*, before gaining the responsibility of a full-length *Panorama* feature.

Peter Bell, the Managing Editor responsible for all BBC Television's daily news and current affairs programmes, says that 'some younger people who prefer to get out of the newsroom and spend time on the road often look to come back indoors in their thirties,' as Senior Producers, Deputy Editors or Programme Editors. Opportunities for young people are increasing in NCA where traditionally the apprenticeship was quite a long one — a recent appointment to the post of Editor of the *Nine O'Clock News* was only 31.

As an indication of its intentions to improve the prospects for women in an area which has traditionally been very much a male preserve, the NCA Directorate has recently appointed its first full-time Equal Opportunities Officer. In a recent count the television newsroom had 30 Assistant Producers, a third of whom were women, and 40 producers, and again a third of these were women. Of the five Programme Editors one was a woman. *Newsnight* has four Senior Producers who work as Editor-of-the-Day, and two of these are women.

The age of entry is usually 25 plus, but may be even 35 plus. The technical skills required have changed somewhat with the arrival of new technology. Shorthand and typing used to be of almost equal importance. The former is always useful, but keyboard skills have become essential because of the universal use of direct-input technology for all scripts, reports and general circulation of news information at all levels.

But Peter Bell thinks that even keyboard skills are less important for would-be recruits than intelligence, knowledge, and a deep interest both in broadcasting and in the world around them. A knowledge of foreign languages is always considered useful.

For his newsgathering production staff Chris Cramer is looking for a high degree of management skills, and the ability to work with large numbers of people in the field. This is more important than, say, knowing the names of all the Cabinet. He is looking for journalistic aptitude, if not experience. He usually takes on new staff in their mid twenties, who he would expect to have reached the level of Duty News Editor by the time they are 30.

By its very nature the work involves irregular hours and shift patterns. These are directly related to the transmission times of the programmes since so much of the output is live, and film and tape reports are being worked on often right up to transmission. The late evening programmes require staff to work longer hours and therefore fewer days than the daytime or early evening ones. In an average week they may work only three or four long days, though because of weekend working the shift patterns are often rostered in fortnights instead of weeks.

The immediacy of the material frequently demands last-minute changes both to the programme content and to the time devoted to producing it. Sudden disasters, natural ones like floods, earthquakes or hurricanes, or man-made such as assassinations or other terrorist outrages, can necessitate swift redeployment of staff to the scene of the tragedy or crime, and the call to work through the night if necessary to bring the story to the public. To meet any eventuality some staff are regularly inoculated for foreign travel, and some always carry their passports and other travel documents with them in case of an emergency departure at a moment's notice.

Other exceptional needs can be anticipated and planned for, like elections or state visits. A general election usually means that most of the team will get very little or even no sleep at all on the night. The last election results programme I worked on went off-air at 4.30 am, and came back on-air at 6.00 am, so I simply showered, changed and went for a brief walk around Television Centre to refresh myself before returning to the studio. I thought an hour's sleep would be worse than none at all. But it is rare for people to work those kind of hours more than occasionally. For those with the right temperament the pressures of big occasions generate so much adrenalin that the excitement or urgency defeats fatigue until it is all over.

The same temperament is needed in news departments elsewhere, but the structures are sometimes different, so it is worth examining them next.

ITN

The 1954 Television Act which established ITV also set up the Independent Television Authority as its regulatory body, which was instructed, among other obligations, to establish a reliable news organisation for the Independent network. So

Independent Television News (ITN) was created as an independent organisation owned by the ITV companies. Ownership may change in the 1990s, but the internal structure of ITN is not likely to change significantly from the present set up, apart from the changes demanded by new technology or new programme outlets on satellite or other channels.

ITN's first news bulletin was presented by Christopher Chataway on 22 September, 1955, and lasted 12 minutes. In 1967 it pioneered the first half-hour news programme in *News at Ten*, using two presenters. In 1972 it introduced lunch-time news with *First Report* which later became *News at One*. In 1976 it added an early evening bulletin in the quarter of an hour running up to 6.00 pm, the time when most of the ITV companies schedule their regional news magazines. Because young children may well be watching at that time, there are certain extra editorial restraints in this bulletin about stories and pictures that they might find disturbing.

The biggest quantum leap yet made by ITN was the introduction of *Channel Four News* on 2 November, 1982. Jeremy Isaacs, the first Chief Executive of Channel 4, and his Senior Commissioning Editor for News and Current Affairs, Liz Forgan, wanted their new channel to have the first hour-long television news programme in Western Europe, and they scheduled it at 7.00 pm, the same point in the evening that the giant networks in America have traditionally run their major news programmes of the day. ITN bid for the commission and won it. An initially uncertain start attracted a barrage of criticism — that it was at the wrong time, with the wrong people, and that many of the stories were too long. But after some unhappy months, and changes of some key staff coupled with a sharpening of its style and journalistic thrust, it has now established itself as a major presence on the television news scene. The greater time at its disposal allows it a flexibility and depth denied to the shorter news programmes, but ITN insists that the production challenge 'is to ensure that the length of an item never becomes a substitute for its depth.'

To meet the demands of all the above programmes, plus several other specialist services for both domestic channels and overseas, by satellite or syndication, ITN employs a staff of nearly a thousand people. 200 of these are journalists, the remainder are technical or production staff fulfilling a variety of roles. There are 50 reporters and 32 ENG crews based at ITN headquarters in Central London. (Electronic News Gathering — shooting on videotape — has now totally replaced film cameras shooting on celluloid for ITN News.) ITN maintains foreign bureaux in Washington, Moscow, South Africa, the Middle East and the Far East, which provide the larger part of its foreign coverage, supplemented by Worldwide Television News (WTN), the international television agency in which the major shareholders are ITN and the American Broadcasting Company.

The usual entry point for new recruits is at the sub-editor, or scriptwriter level, often working with a reporter on the gathering and shaping of a story. Initiative and the ability to write well at speed can lead to Deputy Chief Sub-Editor, or senior scriptwriter, working on the most important or complicated stories. Next comes the Chief Sub (Video), responsible for ensuring that all in-coming pictures are seen, logged, assessed, and then used to their best advantage. This individual must advise the Programme Editor on the picture value of each story, and must know what has been excluded in editing, as well as what is included; and must take a series of key decisions, arbitrate between reporter, scriptwriter and picture editor, and justify recommendations about durations and running orders. Because this figure is constantly on the move in the news area there is another Chief Sub, sometimes described as Chief Sub (Words), who acts as the Programme Editor's deputy, and remains at the desk to handle questions from within the newsroom or from reporters in the field. He or she will check scripts, suggest changes, alter running times, and constantly reshape the programme as events develop or change in relative importance.

The Programme Editor takes the final day-to-day decisions — draws up the list of potential stories after the morning editorial conference, assigns staff to each story, briefs them on the approach and probable duration of each package, and decides the running order and the final shape of each element in it. He or she also has to keep ITN's Editor in touch with developing events where necessary.

That briefly summarises the organisation of the output, but to keep that team supplied there is also the intake side, divided into two desks — Home and Foreign (similar to the BBC structure described earlier).

THE HOME DESK

There are three broad levels of responsibility. The starting level is the Newsdesk Assistant, who calls the various ITV company newsrooms to check their offerings, and deals with routine queries. The News Editor works to the Programme Editor, assigning stories, keeping in touch with them in the field, responding to breaking stories, and advising the Programme Editor on all aspects of immediate home news coverage. Then there is the Senior News Editor, responsible for longer-term coverage, organising reporters and camera crews for special projects for the next day and overall planning for the following week.

THE FOREIGN DESK

This has a very similar set-up. The Foreign Desk Assistant's main function is to participate in the Eurovision link-up conference, representing ITN's interests, and advising on the useful Eurovision offerings to the Foreign Editor. The Foreign Editor's position is analogous to that of the News Editor, presenting a list of foreign stories to the morning conference, collating all the international coverage, arranging incoming satellite feeds, and advising the programme editor on the content of foreign news packages.

The expansion of its output in recent years, and the prospect of further expansion, added to a greater movement between the established news organisations and the newer satellite competitors, has opened up employment prospects at ITN, though not on the same scale as at the BBC. ITN does have a highly regarded traineeship scheme, which lasts for two years, but normally only takes three or four trainees a year, usually university graduates, from a fairly long application list. The Editor of ITN, Stewart Purvis, says he is looking for an informed interest in current affairs. Because the interviews for news trainees often take place around the examination period he often sees applicants who have no idea of what is currently going on in the world, because they have gone into the examination tunnel and shut themselves off from the wider concerns of the day. That is no way to get selected for an ITN News traineeship, as there are often thousands of applications for such a few posts, many of them well thought out, and Stewart Purvis is looking for tangible evidence of that necessary deep interest in, and knowledge of, national and international developments.

He would expect them to have been active in university journalism, to have a good critical view of TV news, both its good and bad points; but the clincher would be having done something about it. In a recent intake he cites the case of Simon Marks, now an ITN reporter, who visited the USA during his time at university and worked on a local station there. He went to Mexico during the earthquake, and rang up TV-AM to offer eye-witness reports.

Most of the ITN staff have done their apprenticeship in the traditional areas, newspapers, regional broadcasting (ITV or BBC), and increasingly radio (including local radio) as much as television. In other words ITN is looking for already established journalistic skills and experience, and the adaptability to pick up quickly the specialist national and international requirements of ITN. This means a starting age of at least 25, and quite often in the early 30s.

When Michael Nicholson applied to ITN straight from university in 1962 he was told to go away and get some experience and come back in a year. So he got a job in the public relations department of the Society of Motor Manufacturers and Traders for four months; and the press experience he gained there helped him to move on to DC Thomsons, the large provincial press and periodicals group, working in Fetter Lane in London as Assistant to the Political Writer, where among other tasks he wrote most of the Diaries for the *Sunday Post*.

Following ITN's advice he re-applied in 1963 and was given a screen test. It was always his ambition to become a reporter, but like everyone else he began as a sub-editor, where he 'started to learn how to write stories,' beginning with how to rewrite the Press Association reports for television. After six months he moved up to Scriptwriter for the voice-over reports on film stories. Eventually he began to narrate his own scripts, and became a reporter after 15 months. He covered a wide variety of domestic stories in his first five years as a reporter, from light colour pieces like Christmas lunch with the homeless to major stories such as the Aberfan disaster, the Torrey Canyon shipwreck, and the Moors Murders. Stewart Purvis comments that the secret of Michael Nicholson's success was that 'he kept offering stories you couldn't say no to'.

He waited four years for his first foreign assignment — Biafra. He arrived in Nigeria the day the Russian tanks rolled into Prague, and feared he was in the wrong place at the wrong time. But his eye-witness reports of what he described as 'genocide' in the Nigerian civil war were the first examples of his journalistic gift for managing to be in exactly the right trouble spot at the right time — in Vietnam, the Jordanian civil war, the Indo-Pakistani war, the Yom Kippur war, the Turkish invasion of Cyprus, the siege of Phnom Penh — 13 war zones in all. In the mid '70s he was ITN's Southern Africa Correspondent where he covered the Soweto riots, and the independence of Mozambique and Angola. In 1978 he was kidnapped by the UNITA rebels in Angola, and neither ITN nor his wife and family knew whether he was alive or dead, until he re-emerged with his camera crew from the bush when he was released four months later. War reporting is a dangerous game; he has won many awards, including the Richard Dimbleby Award for his coverage of the Falklands War, but his life was even more at risk there than in any of the previous wars he had reported.

After nearly three decades of eventful experience, he still regards the reporter's writing skill as the most important requirement, together with a critical appreciation of logistics. His advice is: 'Never come into TV straight away. Get a job first with AP or REUTERS or the PA. The best training is an agency training, beginning by going down the road and asking questions.'

ITV NEWSROOMS

The ladder of advancement in the ITV companies' news and current affairs departments is similar in structure to those already described — sub-editors and researchers to assistant producers, producers and directors, editors, Heads or Controllers of News. That is the production career path, for those either not interested or lacking the presentational skills for an on-screen career as reporter. Reporters and producers have to work closely together, but there is surprisingly little cross-over in either direction.

Traditionally, new entrants to the profession went from school either to a pre-entry course and then into small weekly or daily provincial newspapers, or on to a sandwich course combining their newspaper work with a block-release course, before progressing to radio or television journalism. Or they took the postgraduate route to a large provincial morning or evening newspaper, and on to broadcasting. What used to be a 50:50

ratio of graduates and non-graduates in ITV newsrooms, is now more often around the 70:30 mark, and expected to shift even more to favour those with a degree. This is partly a product of the greater number of graduates on the market, and partly a growing need for highly skilled personnel in all the companies.

A middle-size company like TVS has a staff turnover of between 10 and 15 per cent a year, and recruits externally to three or four posts, but is now moving towards a much heavier use of freelances. Many young people join with the fixed aim of gaining experience and moving on. In one recent 12-month period TVS Current Affairs Department lost two researchers to *World in Action*, two to *This Week*, two to BBC TV News, and two to *Newsnight*. In addition two producers went to *Sky News*, one to Central, one reporter to BBC Belfast, and another to BBC TV News.

The sex ratios are encouraging for women at the younger and/or junior levels — about 50:50 in reporters, and at the Assistant Producer and Producer level about 60:40 male/female. But the senior posts are still held predominantly by men. ITV did have one female Head of News, at Border TV, one of the smallest regional companies, but she has since moved to Sky News.

There has been a slight tendency to downgrade the value of newspaper experience to the television journalist, but this is resisted by Clive Jones, Deputy Director of Programmes at TVS with special responsibility for News and Current Affairs: 'There is a myth that television skills are different from those of the press. This is largely untrue. They both have the same journalistic approach to the gathering of news and the need to co-ordinate its delivery back to the production centre.'

He looks for people who can read fluently, and communicate well, with a proven track record in good quality newspapers or a limited experience in radio journalism. Here too the usual age of entry is around 24/25. A facility for languages can help in the longer term, but Clive Jones is initially looking for other, more specialised qualities: 'A certain amount of brass-neck, a willingness to pick up the 'phone, or to put a foot in the door, an urge to be innovative, an interest in pictures, some kind of visual sense, a machine sense that enables them to cope with the technology, and an ability to think laterally rather than vertically. But for anyone who is a shrinking violet, and shy of people, this is the wrong business to come into.'

He has one final word of warning to those thinking of coming into it: 'Never contemplate it unless you are really sure you want to do it. There is no guarantee you will get to the top.'

SPORT

In ITV Sports Departments are often grouped with News and Current Affairs, so this is probably the best place to say a word about this rather specialist area. One of the most experienced directors of outside broadcasts and many different sports is Bob Gardam, who began his career as an assistant cameraman with the BBC and has since worked for four different ITV companies. He has directed 14 Cup Finals, and has been involved in many major sporting events worldwide. He insists that to succeed you have to have an interest and a true understanding of all sports. 'You have got to live sport.'

Many of those who have reached the pinnacles of achievement in their respective sports necessarily have those qualities and attributes that transfer readily to TV broadcasting, perfect examples being Jimmy Hill, Cliff Morgan, Peter Alliss, John Francome and Richie Benaud. The important thing is that directors have to live the game with the players and understand the pressures they are under. For example, Bob recalls an incident in Italy directing the European Cup Finals when Ron Greenwood, the England Manager, refused to speak to either the press or TV. But on this occasion Bob was able to overcome the barriers which Greenwood had imposed because of the friendship and rapport which they had built up over the years, and secured an exclusive for ITV.

Camera positions can be planned, but the course of the event then dictates the coverage. Some sports are easier than others. Bob Gardam believes that sports that take place within a specific area such as tennis, boxing, football and snooker are relatively straight-forward. 'A Cup Final with 22 cameras and two commentators is not as testing as racing, where there can be as many as seven commentators and frontmen all with specific roles and responsibilities, all of which must blend properly to give the best results. There are only split seconds in which to make the right decision, and an understanding of the rhythm and structure of a day's racing is essential. With horse racing there is often as little as three minutes of racing for an hour's television. This is why it is essential for a producer to work in tandem with the director. His role is to set up interviews and co-ordinate VT inserts and betting-shows while the director is calling the immediate shots. For similar reasons it is essential to have a producer as well for golf, because of the long walks between play.'

One of the most difficult sports to cover is polo, because of the need to use wide shots so much to understand the way the game is going.

The particular need to have an instinctive eye for a picture in covering all sport explains why many successful sports directors are ex-cameramen with a trained eye. The speed of reaction required means it is especially important to mould everyone in the crew into a team. Bob Gardam believes that 80 per cent of directing is motivating the crew to give of their best, in often difficult and trying circumstances. 'Above all, enjoy what you are doing, and maintain a sense of humour. After all, I believe jobs don't come any better!'

Because of the recurring nature of the events through the seasons — FA Cup or League, Test and county matches, Wimbledon, Open Golf, the various race meetings, Rugby Internationals — it is essential to care about the results and the individuals taking part, if this aspect of broadcasting is to prove rewarding.

7

Local radio

I have left until last what is for many young people one of the best places to try first. There are already over 70 ILR and BBC local radio stations, and yet more on the way with the planned expansion into additional community radio stations. The existing stations operate with a small permanent staff of between about 25 and 35 people, but most of them have a high turnover. At BBC Radio Kent, for example, Managing Editor Jim Latham lost 10 out of his 12-strong news team who, he says, 'left for bright lights and loadsamoney'. He has attempted to solve his problems of journalism recruitment by persuading his region to allocate money with which he can fund college bursaries for young people applying for places on vocational radio journalism courses. At present this is attracting more females than males.

The average age is probably lower in any local radio station than in any regional or national centre. This, and the very close links with the local community, produces a much more informal atmosphere than in the larger stations. The small size means a very simple structure. In BBC local radio the overall policy of a station is decided by the Manager or Managing Editor; the day-to-day running of the station is in the hands of his or her deputy, the Programme Organiser; the news output is controlled by the News Editor; and the engineering requirements are in the hands of the Engineer-in-Charge.

Producers can specialise in news, sport, or education, or make general programmes. Recruits in this last-named category frequently come from the ranks of Programme Assistants. Producers in local radio not only devise the programme ideas, and research and gather the material, but also do their own tape-editing, operate the studio and recording equipment, and frequently present the programmes themselves.

News reporters and producers are expected to have at least three years experience of journalism at sub-editor or reporter level, but an appropriate qualification from a radio journalism course may substitute for that requirement for reporters.

Education producers are normally expected to have teaching experience in either the school or further education sectors; their duties include both production and liaison with the local community and educational bodies.

Programme Assistants form the bottom rung of the production ladder, researching material and supporting Producers, and operating the technical equipment on the more complex shows to achieve the correct sound balance. They too will be expected to appear at the microphone, and to combine technical aptitude and manual dexterity with an artistic and creative flair.

They will be expected to play a full part in the work of the station from the day of their arrival, and are likely to gain greater experience more quickly in local radio than anywhere else in broadcasting. Some will enjoy that experience enough to want to stay in this area and end up running their own station, many others see it as a springboard to reaching a wider audience in regional or national broadcasting. The usefulness of such quick experience is recognised by the rest of the system, which has looked increasingly to local radio to discover and develop bright new talent.

Independent Local Radio (ILR) has many of the same characteristics as BBC Local Radio, with some important differences. There are greater variations of size, still averaging around a staff of 30, but with some smaller and a few larger. Some are one-station operations, but quite a number belong to a group, comprising half a dozen or so stations.

The programme mix is geared very much to the needs and tastes of the particular local area. Generalising is particularly difficult in the ILR world, so it is probably more helpful to look at a particular station.

Severn Sound is based in Gloucester, with around 30 full-time staff. Its output is largely made up of entertainment-led news, light music, and some minority programming. In the last three years or so it has moved away from minority programmes in early peak-time, to sequence music programmes throughout the day; the availability of split frequencies allows specific programmes like farming or business to go out on medium wave so that music can continue on VHF.

The newsroom has five staff, engineering two, and administration four. There is a Record Librarian, a commercials production unit of two people, and a Special Projects executive who deals with sponsorship. The production staff has six presenters who each man a sequence; each presenter also has another job — head of music, head of presentation, and so on; these are all full-time staff. But in addition there are eight or nine freelance staff who cover Sundays and specialist programmes. 'Careline' was launched under the sponsorship of the MSC (as it then was), and is run by three full-time staff and many volunteers. There is also a clergyman seconded by the Bishop to liaise with religious organisations, and advise on that element of programming.

There is no particular age-criterion for entry, it is from 18 upwards, and even younger in the clerical area. The production staff came from a number of areas, including other ILR stations, the BBC, and some straight from training courses. There is a high element of cross-pollination with the BBC. When the new BBC local radio station opened in the area the entire Severn Sound newsroom staff apart from the Editor went to join it, which is an indication of the shortage of trained staff (remembering that BBC Radio Kent recently suffered the same loss in the opposite direction). Such a sudden mass exodus tends to redress itself in time, and aids promotion. One girl who joined the Severn Sound newsroom staff from a local newspaper went to the new BBC station as reporter-producer, and has recently rejoined Severn as Editor of News. There is now regular movement between the two local rivals.

Eddie Vickers, Managing Director of Severn Sound, believes this trend will increase, creating much more movement and therefore more vacancies. But he is less convinced that people in his part of the world want to uproot themselves and move on to network radio or television. The geographical attractions of the area are strong, and he says that 'the quality of life is more important than money, people don't always want to move because of money'. He believes that local radio can now offer its own rewarding career path, and has himself come up through local and network radio, been a correspondent abroad, and is now back enjoying running his own local radio station.

His recruitment problem is also the shortage of young talent. He receives about 100 job applications a year and says that any young person with the right qualities and sufficient initiative ought to have no problem getting their foot in the door: 'Listen to your local station, BBC and ILR. Get in touch with the Programme Controller or Programme Organiser. Send in your CV and demo tape, and keep on getting in touch. Ask to go and sit in the newsroom, attach yourself to one of the personnel. There's always some department which will need help or research. Use any way to get in, even if it's not linked to what you eventually want to do, eg join *Careline* to be a newsgatherer and work your way through the station. Sick and relief problems mean there is always a short-term vacancy somewhere or other. Make yourself indispensable to the station.'

That advice is echoed across the ILR network. Heather Purdey at Leicester Sound (part of the Radio Trent Group) also says there is plenty of scope for young people to come in and help out at weekends and evenings. Many stations like to recruit locally because they need local and specialist knowledge. This is particularly true of sport, where many young people help out on Saturdays, and there is quite a cross-over between sport and news. Previous hospital and/or student radio experience is helpful, and there is a growing need for specialist presenters in the ethnic, educational, and arts areas, where a close knowledge and understanding of the subject are of paramount importance. Employment is likely to be initially on a freelance basis, but success can lead to being taken on to the full-time staff. Most presenters however tend to be on freelance contracts.

Others who join on the engineering side may have a specialist interest which can lead to a move into the production side. Record librarians can move on to become Head of Music or Playlist Controllers.

The need for training has become increasingly recognised within the industry, and for ILR this is currently run by Heather Purdey at Leicester Sound, which specialises in short courses:

1 — A two-day weekend course for would-be disc jockeys. This concentrates on the technical skills needed, and real DJs do the training in real studios. Individuals may apply from outside to Leicester Sound, (the fee is £200, plus VAT). Each member of the course makes a half-hour tape, including music presentation, live phone-calls, an interview etc, involving such techniques as talking to time and cueing commercial breaks. The tape may then be used as the demonstration tape for prospective employers.

2 — A four-day course on basic radio skills. The tutors are working journalists and presenters at Leicester Sound, who teach the editorial skills of writing for radio, presenting and

interviewing, the technical skills of dubbing, editing and carting, and the basic principles of broadcast law. Members have to produce a short feature on the last day, as a demonstration tape. (The fee is £250 plus VAT).

3 — A four-day journalist conversion course. This is similar to No 2 (and the same price), but specially designed for print journalists wishing to move into radio, with greater emphasis on news and sport.

4 — There are other ad hoc one- or two-day workshops on specialist aspects of the above, arranged on demand.

Many people in broadcasting have only been on courses after they have gained some practical experience first, and it is usually a help to have picked up some of the basic principles of the particular medium before going on a course. The growing complexity of the business has enhanced the recognition of the need for training at all levels. But in local radio you can break in with nothing but a keen enthusiasm, though to survive and prosper you will need to demonstrate aptitude, intelligence, and original ideas.

Good luck with your chosen route, and I hope you succeed, and enjoy your own broadcasting career as much as I have mine over the last 28 years.

Appendix A

BBC National, Regional and Local Centres

CORPORATE HEADQUARTERS & BBC RADIO

Broadcasting House, London, W1A 1AA
Tel: 01 580 4468

TELEVISION

Television Centre, Wood Lane, London, W12 7RJ
Tel: 01 734 8000

WORLD SERVICE

PO Box 76, Bush House, Strand, London, WC2B 4PH
Tel: 01 240 3456
Monitoring, Caversham Park, Reading, Berkshire, RG4 8TZ
Tel: 0734 472742

OPEN UNIVERSITY PRODUCTION CENTRE

Walton Hall, Milton Keynes, MK7 6BH
Tel: 0908 74033

BBC SCOTLAND

Broadcasting House*, Queen Margaret Drive, Glasgow,
G12 8DG
Tel: 041 330 2345
Broadcasting House, 5 Queen Street, Edinburgh, EH2 1JF
Tel: 031 225 3131
Broadcasting House, Beechgrove Terrace, Aberdeen, AB9 2ZT
Tel: 0224 625233
12-13 Dock Street, Dundee, DD1 4BT
Tel: 0382 25025

(*National or Regional Headquarters)

Community and Area Stations

Radio Aberdeen
Broadcasting House, Beechgrove Terrace, Aberdeen, AB9 2ZT
Tel: 0224 635233
BBC Highland
7 Culduthel Road, Inverness, IV2 4AD
Tel: 0463 221711
BBC Radio nan Gaidheal (Radio nan Eilean)
Rosebank, Church Street, Stornoway, PA87 2LS
Tel: 0851 5000
BBC Radio nan Gaidheal
Clydesdale Bank Buildings, Portree, Skye, IV51 9EH
Tel: 0478 2005
Radio Orkney
Castle Street, Kirkwall, KW15 1DF
Tel: 0856 3939
Radio Shetland
Brentham House, Lerwick, Shetland, ZE1 OLR
Tel: 0595 4747
Radio Solway
Elmbank, Lovers' Walk, Dumfries, DG1 1NZ
Tel: 0387 68008
Radio Tweed
Municipal Buildings, High Street, Selkirk, TD7 4BU
Tel: 0750 21884

BBC WALES

Broadcasting House*, Llantrisant Road, Llandaff, Cardiff,
CF5 2YQ
Tel: 0222 564888
Broadcasting House, Meirion Road, Bangor, Gwynedd,
LL57 2BY
Tel: 0248 362214
32 Alexandra Road, Swansea, SA1 5DZ
Tel: 0792 54986

Community Stations

Radio Clwyd
The Old School House, Glanrafon Road, Mold, Clwyd,
CH7 1PA
Tel: 0352 59111

Radio Gwent
Powys House, Cwmbran, Gwent, NP44 1YF
Tel: 06333 72727

BBC NORTHERN IRELAND

Broadcasting House*, Ormeau Avenue, Belfast, BT2 8HQ
Tel: 0232 244400

Community Station
Radio Foyle
8 Northland Road, Londonderry, BT48 7NE
Tel: 0504 262244/5/6

ENGLISH REGIONS

North West

New Broadcasting House*, Oxford Road, Manchester,
M60 1SJ
Tel: 061 236 8444
Greater Manchester Radio
PO Box 90, New Broadcasting House, Oxford Road,
Manchester, M60 1SJ
Tel: 061 228 3434
Radio Cumbria
Hilltop Heights, London Road, Carlisle, Cumbria, CA1 2NA
Tel: 0228 31661
The address of **Radio Furness**, Cumbria's community opt-out
station, is Broadcasting House, Hartington Street, Barrow-in-
Furness, Cumbria, LA14 5FH Tel: 0229 36767
Radio Lancashire
20-26 Darwen Street, Blackburn, Lancashire, BB2 2EA
Tel: 0254 62411
Radio Merseyside
55 Paradise Street, Liverpool, L1 3BP
Tel: 051 708 5500

North East

BBC Television (Leeds)*
Broadcasting Centre, Woodhouse Lane, Leeds, LS2 9PX
Tel: 0532 441188

BBC Television (Newcastle)
Broadcasting Centre, Barrack Road, Fenham, Newcastle upon Tyne, NE99 2NE
Tel: 091 232 1313
Radio Cleveland
PO Box 1548, Broadcasting House, Newport Road, Middlesborough, Cleveland, TS1 5DG
Tel: 0642 225211
Radio Humberside
63 Jameson Street, Hull, HU1 3NU
Tel: 0482 23232
Radio Leeds
Broadcasting House, Woodhouse Lane, Leeds, LS2 9PN
Tel: 0532 442131
Radio Newcastle
Broadcasting Centre, Barrack Road, Newcastle upon Tyne, NE99 1RN
Tel: 091 232 4141
Radio Sheffield
Ashdell Grove, 60 Westbourne Road, Sheffield, S10 2QU
Tel: 0742 686185
Radio York
20 Bootham Row, York, YO3 7BR
Tel: 0904 641351

Midlands

Broadcasting Centre*, Pebble Mill, Birmingham, B5 7QQ
Tel: 021 414 8888
Radio Derby
56 St Helen's Street, Derby, DE1 3HY
Tel: 0332 361111
Radio Leicester
Epic House, Charles Street, Leicester, LE1 3SH
Tel: 0533 27113
Radio Lincolnshire
PO Box 219, Radion Buildings, Newport, Lincoln, LN1 3XY
Tel: 0522 40011
Radio Nottingham
York House, Mansfield Road, Nottingham, NG1 3JB
Tel: 0602 415161

Radio Shropshire
2-4 Boscobel Drive, Shrewsbury, Shropshire, SY1 3TT
Tel: 0743 248484
Radio Stoke
Conway House, Cheapside, Hanley, Stoke on Trent, ST1 1JJ
Tel: 0782 208080
Radio WM
Broadcasting Centre, Pebble Mill Road, Birmingham,
B5 7SD
Tel: 021 414 8484

South and West

BBC Bristol and BBC West*
Broadcasting House, Whiteladies Road, Bristol, BS8 2LR
Tel: 0272 732211
BBC South
South Western House, Canute Road, Southampton, SO9 1PF
Tel: 0703 226201
BBC South West
Broadcasting House, Seymour Road, Mannamead, Plymouth,
PL3 5BD
Tel: 0752 229201
Radio Bristol
3 Tyndalls Park Road, Bristol, BS8 1PP
Tel: 0272 741111
Somerset Sound
14-15 Paul Street, Taunton, TA1 3PF
Tel: 0823 252437
(Local Radio service opting out of Radio Bristol)
Radio Cornwall
Phoenix Wharf, Truro, Cornwall, TR1 1UA
Tel: 0872 75421
Radio Devon
PO Box 100, St Davids, Exeter, Devon, EX4 4DB
Tel: 0392 215651
Radio Gloucestershire
London Road, Gloucester, GL1 1SW
Tel: 0452 308585
Radio Guernsey
Commerce House, Les Banques, St Peter Port, Guernsey,
Channel Islands
Tel: 0481 28977

Radio Jersey
Broadcasting House, Rouge Bouillon, St Helier, Jersey,
Channel Islands
Tel: 0534 70000
Radio Solent
South Western House, Canute Road, Southampton, SO9 4PJ
Tel: 0703 631311

South and East

BBC South and East*
Elstree Centre, Clarendon Road, Borehamwood, Hertford-
shire, WD6 1JF
Tel: 01 953 6100
BBC East
St Catherine's Close, All Saints Green, Norwich, NR1 3ND
Tel: 0603 619331
Greater London Radio
35a Marylebone High Street, London, W1A 4LG
Tel: 01 486 7611
Radio Bedfordshire
Hastings Street, Luton, Bedfordshire, LU1 5BA
Tel: 0582 459111
Radio Cambridgeshire
Broadcasting House, 104 Hills Road, Cambridge, CB2 1LD
Tel: 0223 315970
BBC Essex
198 New London Road, Chelmsford, Essex, CM2 9AB
Tel: 0245 262393
Radio Kent
Sun Pier, Chatham, Kent ME4 4EZ
Tel: 0634 830505
Radio Norfolk
Norfolk Tower, Surrey Street, Norwich, NR1 3PA
Tel: 0603 617411
Radio Northampton
Abington Street, Northampton, NN1 2BE
Tel: 0604 239100
Radio Oxford
242-254 Banbury Road, Oxford, OX2 7DW
Tel: 0865 53411
Radio Sussex
Marlborough Place, Brighton, East Sussex, BN1 1TU
Tel: 0273 680231

Appendix B

ITV Addresses For Job Applications

Anglia Television
The Personnel Officer, Anglia Television Limited, Anglia
House, Norwich, NR1 3JG
Tel: 0603 615151

Border Television
Personnel Manager, Border Television plc, Television
Centre, Carlisle, CA1 3NT
Tel: 0228 25101

Central Independent Television
Recruitment and Training Officer, Central Independent Television plc, Central House, Broad Street, Birmingham,
B1 2JP
Tel: 021 643 9898
Recruitment and Training Officer, Central Independent Television plc, East Midlands Television Centre, Lenton Lane,
Nottingham, NG7 2NA
Tel: 0602 863322

Channel Television
Secretary to the Managing Director, Channel Television,
The Television Centre, St Helier, Jersey, Channel Islands
Tel: 0534 73999
(NB Channel Television is unable to offer employment to
persons who are not qualified as Channel Islands residents
under the Jersey and Guernsey housing regulations.)

Grampian Television
The Personnel Officer, Grampian Television plc, Queen's
Cross, Aberdeen, AB9 2XJ
Tel: 0224 646464

Granada Television
The Personnel Manager, Granada Television Limited, Quay Street, Manchester, M60 9EA
Tel: 061 832 7211
Personnel Officer, Granada Group Limited, 36 Golden Square, London W1R 4AH
Tel: 01 734 8080

HTV
The Personnel Manager, HTV Wales, The Television Centre, Culverhouse Cross, Cardiff, CF5 6XJ
Tel: 0222 590590
HTV West
Television Centre, Bath Road, Bristol, BS4 3HG
Tel: 0272 778366
HTV Wales
Television Centre, Mold, Clwyd, CH7 1YA
Tel: 0352 55331
(NB All applications for jobs should be sent to Cardiff.)

Independent Television News
The Personnel Manager, Independent Television News Limited, ITN House, 48 Wells Street, London, W1P 4DE
Tel: 01 637 2424

London Weekend Television
The Personnel Manager, London Weekend Television Limited, South Bank Television Centre, Kent House, Upper Ground, London, SE1 9LT
Tel: 01 261 3434

Scottish Television
The Recruitment and Training Manager, Scottish Television plc, Cowcaddens, Glasgow, G2 3PR
Tel: 041 332 9999

TSW — Television South West
The Personnel Manager, TSW — Television South West Limited, Derry's Cross, Plymouth, PL1 2SP
Tel: 0752 663322

Thames Television
The Controller of Personnel, Thames Television Limited, Teddington Studios, Teddington Lock, Teddington, Middlesex, TW11 9NT
Tel: 01 977 3252
The Senior Personnel Officer, Thames Television Limited, Thames Television House, 306-316 Euston Road, London, NW1 3BB
Tel: 01 387 9494

TV AM
The Personnel Administrator, Breakfast Television Centre, Hawley Crescent, London, NW1 8EF
Tel: 01 267 4300

TVS (Television South)
The Personnel and Recruitment Manager, TVS, Television Centre, Northam, Southampton, SO9 5HZ
Tel: 0703 634211
Personnel Manager, TVS, Television Centre, Vinters Park, Maidstone, Kent, ME14 5TT
Tel: 0622 691111

Tyne Tees Television
The Personnel Manager, Tyne Tees Television Limited, The Television Centre, City Road, Newcastle upon Tyne, NE1 2AL
Tel: 0632 610181

Ulster Television
The Personnel Manager, Ulster Television Limited, Havelock House, Ormeau Road, Belfast, BT7 1EB
Tel: 0232 228122

Yorkshire Television
The Personnel Executive, Yorkshire Television Limited, The Television Centre, Leeds, LS3 1JS
Tel: 0532 438283

Where To Look For Job Advertisements
Some publications which carry job advertisements for Independent Television are: *The Guardian* Media Page, *Broadcast*, *Campaign* (Sales and Marketing Posts), *Sight and*

Sound, Stage and Television Today, Audio Visual (technical posts), *UK Press Gazette,* and appropriate technical and hobby publications. Advertisements are also placed in the national and local press.

Jobs for engineers are advertised in a wide range of professional and technical journals.

Many of the specialist publications are available in newsagents in London's West End, but elsewhere they may only be available on special order through newsagents, or at local libraries.

Appendix C

Independent Local Radio Stations

Radio Aire — Leeds
PO Box 362, Leeds, LS3 1LR
Tel: 0532 452299

**Beacon Radio — Wolverhampton and Black Country /
Shrewsbury and Telford**
267 Tettenhall Road, Wolverhampton, WV6 ODQ
Tel: 0902 757211
Thorns Hall, 28 Castle Street, Shrewsbury, SY2 2BQ
Tel: 0743 232271

BRMB Radio — Birmingham
Radio House, PO Box 555, Aston Road North, Birmingham,
B6 4BX
Tel: 021 359 4481/9

Radio Broadland — Norwich and Great Yarmouth
St George's Plain, 47-49 Colegate, Norwich, NR3 1DB
Tel: 0603 630621

Capital Radio — London — General and Entertainment
Euston Tower, London, NW1 3DR
Tel: 01 388 1288

Chiltern Radio — Luton/Bedford
Chiltern Road, Dunstable, LU6 1HQ
Tel: 0582 666001
55 Goldington Road, Bedford, MK40 3LS
Tel: 0234 272400

Radio City — Liverpool
PO Box 967, Liverpool, L69 1TQ
Tel: 051 227 5100

Radio Clyde — Glasgow
Clydebank Business Park, Clydebank, Glasgow, G81 2RX
Tel: 041 941 1111

CN.FM — Cambridge and Newmarket
PO Box 1000, The Vision Park, Chivers Way, Histon, Cambridge CB4 4WW
Tel: 0223 235255

County Sound Radio — Guildford
Chertsey Road, Woking, GU21 5XY
Tel: 0483 740066

Devonair Radio — Exeter/Torbay
35-37 St David's Hill, Exeter, EX4 4DA
Tel: 0392 30703

Downtown Radio — Belfast/Londonderry/Enniskillen and Omagh
PO Box 96, Newtownards, County Down, Northern Ireland, BT23 4ES
Tel: 0247 815555

Essex Radio — Southend/Chelmsford
Radio House, Clifftown Road, Southend-on-Sea, SS1 1SX
Tel: 0702 333711

Radio Forth — Edinburgh
Forth House, Forth Street, Edinburgh, EH1 3LF
Tel: 031 556 9255

GWR Radio — Bristol/Swindon/West Wiltshire
PO Box 2000, Bristol, BS99 7SN
Tel: 0272 279900
PO Box 2000, Swindon, SN4 7EX
Tel: 0793 853222

Radio Hallam — Part of the Yorkshire Radio Network — Sheffield and Rotherham/Barnsley/Doncaster
PO Box 194, Sheffield, S1 1GP
Tel: 0742 766766

Hereward Radio — Peterborough
PO Box 225, Queensgate Centre, Peterborough, PE1 1XJ
Tel: 0733 46225

Horizon Radio — Part of the Chiltern Network — Milton Keynes
Unit 7, Crownhill Business Park, Vincent Avenue, Milton Keynes
Tel: 0908 269111

Independent Radio News (IRN) — see below

Invicta Radio — Maidstone and Medway/East Kent
15 Station Road East, Canterbury, CT1 2RB
Tel: 0227 67661
37 Earl Street, Maidstone, ME14 1PF
Tel: 0622 679061
Unit 210, Medway Enterprise Centre, Enterprise Close, Strood, Rochester, ME2 4LY
Tel: 0634 719400

LBC (London Broadcasting Company) — London — News and Information
Communications House, Gough Square, London, EC4P 4LP
Tel: 01 353 1010

Leicester Sound — Leicester
Granville House, Granville Road, Leicester, LE1 7RW
Tel: 0533 551616

Marcher Sound — Wrexham and Deeside
The Studios, Mold Road, Gwersyllt, Wrexham, Clwyd, LL11 4AF
Tel: 0978 752202

Mercia Sound — Coventry
Hertford Place, Coventry, CV1 3TT
Tel: 0203 633933

Radio Mercury — Reigate & Crawley
Broadfield House, Brighton Road, Crawley, West Sussex, RH11 9TT
Tel: 0293 519161

Metro Radio — Tyne and Wear
Long Rigg, Swalwell, Newcastle-upon-Tyne, NE99 1BB
Tel: 091 488 3131

Moray Firth Radio — Inverness
PO Box 271, Inverness, IV3 6SF
Tel: 0463 224433

**Northants 96 — Part of the Chiltern Network —
Northampton**
71b Abington Street, Northampton, NN1 2HW
Tel: 0604 29811

Northsound Radio — Aberdeen
45 King's Gate, Aberdeen, AB2 6BL
Tel: 0224 632234

Ocean Sound — Portsmouth/Southampton/Winchester
Whittle Avenue, Segensworth West, Fareham, Hampshire,
PO15 5PA
Tel: 0489 589911

Orchard FM — Yeovil/Taunton
Haygrove House, Shoreditch, Taunton, Somerset, TA3 7BT
Tel: 0460 52963

Radio Orwell — Ipswich
Electric House, Lloyds Avenue, Ipswich, IP1 3HZ
Tel: 0473 216971

**Pennine Radio — Part of the Yorkshire Network —
Bradford/Huddersfield and Halifax**
PO Box 235, Pennine House, Forster Square, Bradford,
BD1 5NP
Tel: 0274 731521

Piccadilly Radio — Manchester
127/131 The Piazza, Piccadilly Plaza, Manchester, M1 4AW
Tel: 061 236 9913

Plymouth Sound — Plymouth
Earl's Acre, Plymouth, PL3 4HX
Tel: 0752 227272

Red Dragon Radio — Cardiff/Newport
Radio House, West Canal Wharf, Cardiff, CF1 5XJ
Tel: 0222 384041

Red Rose Radio — Preston and Blackpool
PO Box 301, St. Paul's Square, Preston, PR1 1YE
Tel: 0772 556301

Saxon Radio — Bury St Edmunds
Long Brackland, Bury St Edmunds, Suffolk, IP33 1JY
Tel: 0284 701511

Severn Sound — Gloucester and Cheltenham
PO Box 388, 67 Southgate Street, Gloucester, GL1 2DQ
Tel: 0452 423791

Signal Radio — Stoke-on-Trent
Studio 257, Stoke Road, Stoke-on-Trent, ST4 2SR
Tel: 0782 747047

Southern Sound Radio — Brighton
Radio House, PO Box 2000, Brighton, Sussex, BN41 2SS
Tel: 0273 430111
Radio House, PO Box 2000, Eastbourne, Sussex, BN21 4UH
Tel: 0323 430111

Swansea Sound — Swansea
Victoria Road, Gowerton, Swansea, SA4 3AB
Tel: 0792 893751/6

Radio Tay — Dundee/Perth
PO Box 123, Dundee, DD1 9UF
Tel: 0382 200800

TFM Radio — Teeside
74 Dovecot Street, Stockton-on-Tees, Cleveland, TS18 1HB
Tel: 0642 615111

Radio Trent — Nottingham/Derby
29-31 Castle Gate, Nottingham, NG1 7AP
Tel: 0602 581731

Two Counties Radio(2CR) — Bournemouth
5-7 Southcote Road, Bournemouth, BH1 3LR
Tel: 0202 294881

Radio 210 — Reading/Basingstoke and Andover
PO Box 210, Reading, Berkshire, RG3 5RZ
Tel: 0734 413131

**Viking Radio — Part of the Yorkshire Radio Network
— Humberside**
Commercial Road, Hull, HU1 2SG
Tel: 0482 25141

West Sound — Ayr
Radio House, Holmston Road, Ayr, KA7 3BE
Tel: 0292 283662

Radio Wyvern — Hereford/Worcester
5-6 Barbourne Terrace, Worcester, WR1 3JS
Tel: 0905 612212

Independent Radio News (IRN)
Communications House, Gough Square, London, EC4P 4LP
Tel: 01 353 1010

In 1989 the IBA awarded additional Incremental Contracts for a period up to December 1994, when the
last of the IBA's existing radio contracts expires.
These new incremental stations will provide programming directed towards 'communities of interest',
including ethnic groups and specialist music interests, or small geographical communities. The successful groups were:

Belfast (VHF/FM)
Belfast Community Radio
28 Bedford Street, Belfast, BT2 7FE
Tel: 0232 483500

Birmingham (VHF/FM)
Buzz FM
King Edward Building, 205-219 Corporation Street,
Birmingham, B4 6SE
Tel: 021 236 0258

Bradford (VHF/FM ethnic)
Bradford City Radio
30 Chapel Street, Little Germany, Bradford, BD1 5DN
Tel: 0274 735043

Bristol (VHF/FM)
FTP (For the People)
30 Nevil Road, Bishopston, Bristol, BS7 9EQ
Tel: 0272 243286

Brixton (VHF/FM, ethnic)
Choice FM
28A Enford Street, London, W1H 1DG
Tel: 01 706 1619

Coventry (VHF/FM, ethnic)
Radio Harmony
353 Pershore Road, Edgbaston, Birmingham, B5 7RY
Tel: 021 472 0310

Easterhouse (East Glasgow) (VHF/FM)
East End Radio
The Greater Easterhouse Business Centre, Unit 16, 19
Blairtummock Road, Queensile Industrial Estate, Glasgow,
G33 4AN
Tel: 041 771 9759 or 041 3324946

Greater London (Medium Wave/AM, multi-ethnic)
Spectrum Radio
11 Byron Road, London, NW7 4AH
Tel: 01 229 2244

Greater London (VHF/FM, Community of interest)
Jazz FM
26/27 Castlereagh Street, London, W1H 5YR
Tel: 01 402 2191

Kiss FM
14 Blackstock Mews, 100 Blackstock Road, London, N4 2DR
Tel: 01 359 2969 or 01 487 4284
Melody Radio
1 Grosvenor Place, London, SW1X 7JH
Tel: 01 245 1245 or 041 941 1111

Haringey (VHF/FM, ethnic)
Airtime to be shared equally, as proposed by the applicants, between:
London Greek Radio
Florentia Village, Vale Road, London N4 1TD
Tel: 01 800 8001
and
W.N.K. Radio
185B High Road, Wood Green, London, N22 6BA
Tel: 01 889 1547

Heathrow/Gatwick Airports (Medium Wave/AM)
Airport Information Radio Ltd
Broadfield House, Brighton Road, Crawley, West Sussex, RH11 9TT
Tel: 0293 519161

Hounslow/Ealing/Southall (Medium Wave/AM ethnic)
Sunrise Radio
5 The Crescent, Southall, Middlesex, UB1 1BE
Tel: 01 569 6666

Isle of Wight (Medium Wave/AM)
Isle of Wight Radio
16A High Street, Newport, Isle of Wight, PO33 1SS
Tel: 0983 822557

Kettering (Medium Wave/AM)
KNBC Radio
Unit 1, Centre 2000, Robinson Close, Kettering, Northamptonshire, NN16 8PU
Tel: 0536 410723

Manchester (VHF/FM, ethnic)
Sunset Radio
23 New Mount Street, Manchester, M4 4DE
Tel: 061 953 5333

Stirling (VHF/FM)
Centresound
Stirling Enterprise Park, John Player Building, Kerse Road, Stirling, FK7 7RP
Tel: 0786 51188

Stockport (VHF/FM)
KFM Radio
Regent House, Heaton Lane, Stockport, SK4 1BX
Tel: 061 4805445

Sunderland (VHF/FM)
Sunderland Community Radio Association
53 Frederick Street, Sunderland, SR1 1NF
Tel: 091 5651566

Tendring (Medium Wave/AM)
26 Orwell Road, Clacton-on-sea, Essex
Tel: 0255 221777

Thamesmead
RTM (Independent Radio Thamesmead)
19 Tavy Bridge, Thamesmead, London, SE2 9UG
Tel: 01 311 3112

West Lothian
Community Radio Association West Lothian (CRAWL)
28 Athol Terrace, Bathgate, West Lothian, EH48 4DF
Tel: 0506 630227

Appendix D

Educational Institutions Which Run Courses Relevant To Broadcasting

Bournemouth and Poole College of Art and Design
Wallisdown Road, Poole, Dorset, BH12 5HH
Tel: 0202 533011

Bristol Polytechnic
Postgraduate Admissions Office, Coldharbour Lane, Frenchay, Bristol, BS16 1QY
Tel: 0272 656261

Croydon College
School of Art and Design, Fairfield, Croydon, Surrey, CR9 1DX
Tel: 01 686 5700

Cyfle
Maesinda, Caernarvon, Gwynedd, LL55 1NW
Tel: 0286 671000

Dorset Institute
Wallisdown Road, Poole, Dorset, BH12 5BB
Tel: 0202 524111

Duncan of Jordanstone College of Art
13 Perth Road, Dundee, DD1 4HT
Tel: 0382 23261

Glasgow School of Art
167 Renfrew Street, Glasgow, G3 6RQ
Tel: 041 332 9797

Gwent College of Further Education
Faculty of Art and Design, Film School, Clarence Place, Newport, Gwent, NP9 OUW
Tel: 0633 259984

Harrow College of Art and Design
Faculty of Arts and Photography, Film and TV School, Watford Road, Northwick Park, Harrow, Middlesex, HA1 3TT
Tel: 01 864 5422

Howard Steele Foundation
Chalfont Grove, Gerrards Cross, Buckinghamshire, SL9 8TN
Tel: 02407 5982

Humberside College of Higher Education
Schools of Visual Communication, Design and Fine Art, Queens Gardens, Hull, North Humberside, HU1 2DH
Tel:0482 224121

Jobfit*
4th Floor, 5 Dean Street, London, W1V 5RN
Tel: 01 734 5141

Kingston Polytechnic
Penryn Road, Kingston upon Thames, Surrey, KT1 2EE
Tel: 01 549 1366

Leeds Polytechnic
School of Creative Arts and Design, Calverly Street, Leeds, LS1 3HE
Tel: 0532 832600

Liverpool Polytechnic
Arts, Media and Design, 68 Hope Street, Liverpool, L1 9EB
Tel: 051 207 3581

London College of Printing*
Elephant and Castle, London, SE1 6SB
Tel: 01 735 9100

London International Film School*
24 Shelton Street, London, WC2H 9HP
Tel: 01 240 0168

London Video Arts
23 Frith Street, London, W1V 5TS
Tel: 01 734 7410 / 01 437 2786

Manchester Polytechnic
Department of Communication, Art and Design, Capital
Building, School Lane, Didsbury, Manchester, M20 OHT
Tel: 061 434 3331

Middlesex Polytechnic
Art and Design Faculty Office, Cat Hill, Barnet, Hertford-
shire, EN4 8HT
Tel: 01 440 5181

National Film and Television School*
Beaconsfield Studios, Station Road, Beaconsfield, Bucking-
hamshire, HP9 1LG
Tel: 04946 71234

**Polytechnic of Central London School of Communica-
tion***
18-22 Riding House Street, London, W1P 7PD
Tel: 01 486 5811

Plymouth College of Art and Design
Department of Photography, Tavistock Place, Plymouth,
PL4 8AT
Tel: 0752 264774

Ravensbourne College of Design and Communication
Department of Television, 3 Wharton Road, Bromley, Kent
BR1 3LE
Tel: 01 468 7071

Royal College of Art
School of Film and Television, Kensington Gore, London,
SW7 2EU
Tel: 01 584 5020

Saint Martin's School of Art
Film and Video Unit, 27-29 Long Acre, London, WC2E 9LA
Tel: 01 437 0611

Scottish Film Training Trust
Dowanhill, 74 Victoria Crescent Road, Glasgow, G12 9JN
Tel: 041 334 9314

Sheffield City Polytechnic
Faculty of Art and Design, Brincliffe, Psalter Lane, Sheffield, S11 8UZ
Tel: 0742 556101

Suffolk College
Department of Art and Design, High Street, Ipswich,
IP1 3QH
Tel: 0473 55885

Sunderland Polytechnic
Centre for Continuing Education, 3 Greens Terrace, Sunderland, SR1 3PZ
Tel: 091 515 2925

University of Bristol*
29 Park Road, Bristol, BS1 5LT
Tel: 0272 303030

University of Glasgow
The Registrar, University of Glasgow, Glasgow, G12 8QQ
Tel: 041 339 8855

University of London
Higher Degrees Office, University Road, Leicester, LE1 7RH
Tel: 0533 522298

University of Hull
Postgraduate Office, University of Hull, Hull, HU6 7RX
Tel: 0482 46311

West Surrey College of Art and Design*
Falkner Road, The Hart, Farnham, Surrey, GU9 7DS
Tel: 0252 722441

* indicates ACTT Accreditation

Appendix E

Recognised Journalism Courses

London College of Printing
Elephant and Castle, London, SE1 6SB
Tel: 01 735 9100
Periodical Journalism — one-year, pre-entry course; one-term postgraduate course; HND business studies (periodical journalism option in second year).
Radio Journalism — postgraduate/mature students' one-year CNAA diploma course.

Harlow College
Journalism Division, Harlow College, East Site, The Hides, Netteswell, Harlow, Essex, CM20 3RA
Tel: 0279 441288
Newspaper journalism — one-year, pre-entry course.

Highbury College of Technology
Cosham, Portsmouth, Hampshire, PO6 2SA
Tel: 0705 383131
Newspaper Journalism — one-year, pre-entry course.
Radio Journalism* — one-year, postgraduate pre-entry course.

College of Business Studies
Brunswick Street, Belfast BT2 7GX
Tel: 0232 245891
Newspaper Journalism — one-year, pre-entry course.

PMA Publishing Services Limited
PMA Training, The Old Anchor, Church Street, Hemingford Grey, Huntingdon, Cambridgeshire PE18 9DF
Tel: 0480 300 653
Periodical and Radio Journalism — short courses.

Napier College
Department of Print, Media, Publishing and Communications, 219 Colinton Road, Edinburgh, EH14 1DJ
Tel: 031 444 2266
HND Journalism Studies — two-year course covering journalism across the media: newspapers, broadcasting, etc.

London College of Fashion
20 John Princes Street, London, W1M 0BJ
Tel: 01 629 9401
HND Fashion Design — two-year course with Fashion Writing option over whole course.

University College
Centre for Journalism Studies, PO Box 78, 69 Park Place, Cardiff, CF1 1XL
Tel: 0222 874786
Postgraduate Journalism Diploma course — one-year course with full broadcasting (Radio/TV) option.

City University
Northampton Square, London, EC1
Tel: 01 253 4399
Postgraduate Newspaper Journalism course — one-year course.
Postgraduate Radio Journalism course — one-year course.
Postgraduate Periodical Journalism course — one-year course.

Richmond College of Further Education
Spinkhill Drive, Sheffield, South Yorkshire, S13 8FD
Tel: 0742 392612
Newspaper Journalism — one-year, pre-entry course.
Press Photography — one-year, pre-entry course.

South Glamorgan Institute of Higher Education
Colchester Avenue, Cardiff, CF1 7XR
Tel: 0222 551111
Newspaper Journalism — one-year, pre-entry course; 18-week graduate pre-entry course.

College of Technology
Cleveland Avenue, Darlington, County Durham DL3 7BB
Tel: 0325 467651
Newspaper Journalism — one-year, pre-entry course.
International Diploma in Journalism — one-year course for students from overseas.

Lancashire Polytechnic
Colonial Buildings, Preston, Lancashire, PR1 2TQ
Tel: 0772 201201
Newspaper Journalism — one-year, pre-entry course.
Radio Journalism* — one-year, postgraduate pre-entry course.

Falmouth Centre
Cornwall College of Further and Higher Education, Killigrew Street, Falmouth, Cornwall, TR11 3Q3
Tel: 9326 313326
Radio Journalism* — one-year, postgraduate pre-entry course.

Polytechnic of Central London
School of Communication, 18-22 Riding House Street, London, W1P 7PD
Tel: 01 404 5353
Radio Journalism — one-year, pre-entry course for ethnic minority students.

REPUBLIC OF IRELAND

College of Commerce
Rathmines Road, Dublin 6, Republic of Ireland
Tel: 0001 985412
Newspaper Journalism — two-year, pre-entry course.

National Institute for Higher Education
Dublin 9, Republic of Ireland
Tel: 0001 370077
Journalism (including broadcast journalism, both radio and television) — one-year postgraduate course.

JOURNALISM TRAINING ORGANISATIONS

Periodical Journalism

Periodical Training Centre
Imperial House, 15-19 Kingsway, London, WC2B 6UN
Tel: 01 836 8798

Press and Public Relations

Institute of Public Relations
1 Great James Street, London, WC1
Tel: 01 253 5151
British Association of Industrial Editors
3 Lock's Yard, High Street, Sevenoaks, Kent, TN13 1LT
Tel: 0732 459331

Overseas Students

The Thomson Foundation
Regent's College, Inner Circle, Regent's Park, London, NW1 4NS
Tel: 01 487 7408

Newspaper Journalism

National Council for the Training of Journalists
Carlton House, Hemnall Street, Epping, Essex, CM16 4NL
Tel: 0378 72395

Radio Journalism

Joint Advisory Committee for Radio Journalism Training
c/o National Union of Journalists, Acorn House, 314 Gray's Inn Road, London, WC1X 8DP
Tel: 01 278 7916

* These courses, whilst mainly postgraduate, will consider non-graduate applicants.